IN DEFENSE OF

FOOD CONTROVERSIES

SERIES EDITOR: ANDREW F. SMITH

Everybody eats. Yet few understand the importance of food
in our lives and the decisions we make each time we eat.
The Food Controversies series probes problems created by
the industrial food system and examines proposed alternatives.

Already published:

IN DEFENSE OF PROCESSED FOOD

ANASTACIA MARX DE SALCEDO

REAKTION BOOKS

To Jorge, who has taught me to appreciate so many,
many things

Published by Reaktion Books Ltd
Unit 32, Waterside
44–48 Wharf Road
London N1 7UX, UK
www.reaktionbooks.co.uk

First published 2023
Copyright © Anastacia Marx de Salcedo 2023

Printed and bound in Great Britain by Bell & Bain, Glasgow

A catalogue record for this book is available from the British Library

ISBN 978 1 78914 767 4

CONTENTS

INTRODUCTION

Dinner at my house is a guilt-inducing affair. A couple days a week, I cook from scratch, or we do take-out, mostly pizza from the Algerian place down the street. But most nights I ransack my fridge and pantry for bags, boxes, bottles, and cans from the supermarket to quickly open, heat, and serve. I do so with a pang, since I, like many, believe these products are a devil's bargain. What we gain in convenience, we lose in healthfulness, as they are laden with sugar, salt, and chemical additives. Moreover, I cannot help but feel I am somehow gypping my children of the homemade meal that quarters as disparate as the White House, the Academy of Nutrition and Dietetics, the American Medical Association, the American Academy of Pediatrics, the National Center on Addiction and Substance Abuse, Slow Food International, and even the Vatican tell me is their birthright. And finally let's not forget my heedless support of giant agribusiness and international conglomerates in lieu of the small, local farms and food producers whose colorful wares are on display at any outdoor market or independent store.

The family dinner has become the answer—perhaps the only one agreed upon by conservatives and liberals alike—to almost every modern ill: obesity, diabetes, cancer, giant agri-businesses, predatory conglomerates, disappearing family farms, shuttered main street businesses, environmental degradation, and the adolescent quadruple whammy of depression, poor grades, drug and alcohol abuse, and pregnancy. And, unlike many solutions, it doesn't entail getting a bunch of quarrelsome legislators to agree on a policy and then, even more quarrelsomely, to fund it. Yet these calls to get busy in the kitchen blithely omit a central fact.

Cooking and cleaning up after meals take time—52 minutes daily, and most of that time is spent by women: about 72 percent overall, according to the U.S. Census Bureau's 2021 American Time Use Survey (ATUS). Those numbers shoot up when there are children in the home to an average of 63 minutes, according to ATUS, and 80 percent of women, shows a 2011 United States Department of Agriculture (USDA) study. The gender imbalance gapes to 100 percent when it comes to worrying. "Although both mothers and fathers reported feeling rushed, stressed, and tired . . . only mothers reported feeling guilty how competing demands had influenced their food coping strategies," Cornell nutrition and public health researchers find.

Which gives rise to scenarios like the following: up before dawn to get the kids ready for school, drive to work, work, drive home, ferry children to and from various activities, do a fill-in shopping, start a load of laundry, tidy undone breakfast dishes . . . And then pump out a gourmet repast of roasted salmon glazed with brown sugar and mustard, celery-root potato purée and charred broccoli (*New York Times*). Or, in the morning as you're assembling sandwiches for a line of lunch boxes, simultaneously fire up the crockpot with chicken, potatoes, carrots, celery, and dumplings in a cream sauce (Rachael Ray). Or turn the whole thing into family together time by insisting that at 6 p.m. everyone file into the kitchen to roll out and stuff pepperoni pizza pockets (The Food Network). These well-meaning suggestions by food writers—often male—would sound a lot less well-meaning if they described the real-life context in which these dishes are frequently made. While your partner is splayed on the couch watching TV/checking email/tweeting and the kids are upstairs in their bedrooms playing video games/posting to Instagram/texting, the lady of the house shall sequester herself in the kitchen to concoct the evening sustenance. (Is it mean-spirited to observe that these gurus are professionals paid to write about cooking and that they have a vested interest in expanding their audience?) But before we ditch the from-scratch dinner as an affront to modern feminism, let's reconsider an option long vilified by foodies and public health activists: processed food.

My argument for the use of processed foods has four parts: scientific, social, economic, and medical. This book will make the case that the glorification of home-cooked meals, the default position of most food and health activists, is based on a misguided understanding of how modern industrial food is made; is actively detrimental to women's equality; is a drag on community service and national economic progress, no matter the income level of the country; and is highly unlikely to arrest the worldwide epidemic of cardiovascular and metabolic diseases most often attributed to obesity.

After probing what processed food really is and describing its history in the first chapter, the second chapter will cover new food science that contributes to making modern processed food more healthful—fewer additives, less salt and sugar, and better retention of vitamins and nutrients. The third chapter will examine how cooking factors into women's use of time, in wealthy and middle- and low-income countries, and how these demands affect their ability to study, work, volunteer, and be politically active. The fourth chapter will look at food-related careers' impact on altruism, especially among young people, and scrutinize national economic data from around the world, showing that the wealthier a country is, the smaller the proportion of business and employment classifications related to agriculture, food processing, and food service. The final chapter will revisit the obesity and lifestyle disease epidemic, tease apart the different factors medical experts believe contribute, and conclude that food has been overemphasized, while others—access to medical care and physical activity—have been downplayed.

NOTE: To protect people's privacy, names and some details have been changed in the sections that include personal anecdotes.

1

WHAT IS PROCESSED FOOD?

Lisa Leake, the force of nature behind the blog 100 Days of Real Food, a popular cookbook series, and a killer Instagram product placement platform (Handzies Wipes, Nick's Sticks jerky, NovaFuse aromatherapy, and so on), had her come-to-Jesus moment after hearing about Michael Pollan's book *In Defense of Food* on Oprah and then reading it. "Processed foods are an illusion, often appearing to be healthy . . . when these foods are in fact the very thing making a lot of Americans unhealthy, sick, and fat," she says. Not only that but "four of the top ten chronic diseases that kill most of us 'can be traced directly to the industrialization of our food,' according to Michael Pollan." After seeing the light in 2010, the stay-at-home mother of two from Matthews, North Carolina, vowed to feed her family only "real food" for three and a half months.

Which meant excluding what exactly? For most people, the terms "real food" and "processed food" seem to be opposites. Yet Leake and others grope to explain exactly what processed food is. Leake describes it, variously, as food that is "scientifically designed never to rot," "up to 90 percent . . . contains either a corn or soy ingredient in the form of an additive under a variety of different names," and full of unpronounceable ingredients of mysterious origin. Chowhound.com message-board users echo her talking points:

[P]seudo-foods—I call them "pfood"s—consisting of man-made ingredients that were created in a lab.
—goodhealthgourmet

Whether it's "processed" depends on how recognizable it is (the shorter the ingredients list the better) and how many different treatments it's had to go through to get to you . . . [T]he more they mess with it, the worse it gets.
—Kajikit

I think Michael Pollan put it best . . . if your great-grandmother wouldn't have recognized it as food, you probably shouldn't eat it.
—BarmyFotheringayPhipps

[C]hemical-laden foods that can sit on store shelves or in your fridge for months on end without growing mold.
—RosemaryHoney

The term "processed food" tends to conjure up visions of sofa surfers awash in Flamin' Hot Cheetos and Mountain Dew, but ready-to-eat snack foods are just one of its many categories. These include items as varied as bagged salad greens, canned green beans, and frozen collards; needled, or mechanically tenderized meat kept cherry-red in its package with carbon monoxide, frozen hamburger patties or "preservative-free" deli meat made with high-pressure processing; milk, yogurt, and cheese; almost any condiment; and every single individual item in the ingredients you combine for your "homemade" spaghetti dinner. Technically, any food that has had something done to it before eating is a processed food.

Food processing is ancient; it predates our species and could even be considered a characteristic primate behavior, since many monkeys and apes use their hands and brains to improve the edibility and digestibility of what they consume. We humans have, of course, taken this to an extreme. From the days when *Homo erectus* first hunted with spears and dug up tubers with sticks, our library of culinary implements and methods has continually grown, allowing us to eat just about everything on the planet: plant, animal, or mineral (and fungus and bacterium).

When we found something we couldn't choke down in its raw state, we mixed and matched processing techniques until we ended up with something delectable far from its natural form. What else could explain capers (pickled buds); saffron (dried flower stamens); fish sauce (fermented fish parts); jaggary, traditional Indian sugar (crushed, boiled sugarcane plants); coffee (the seeds of tiny dried "cherries" that are removed, aged, roasted, ground, and infused in hot water); tofu (soy beans that are dried, ground, soaked to create a milk, solids coagulated with an acid, and finally pressed to form firm cakes); and that tour de force, bread (seeds that have been dried, ground, mixed with water to form a paste, fermented, and baked)?

Many of these processes were created by applying our ever-expanding knowledge of practical, if not theoretical, science. Water-powered gristmills to grind grain were reportedly in use more than two millennia ago in Turkey, and stills for purifying water and other beverages in fourth-century Egypt. (And all this is *before* the industrial and chemical revolutions.) These traditional foodstuffs and many more are frequently concocted with ingredients not readily found in nature, may involve multiple processes, and can last for a very long time. These are the exact same objections people make to modern processed food. (Which leads me to the conclusion that it isn't the food processing that people object to, but the entry of science and industry into the kitchen.)

While food processing itself has a long pedigree, the term "processed food" is a scrappy newcomer. It arose in the throes of a vicious food fight—one that may have helped trigger the 1929 stock market crash. After the First World War, buoyed by the high price their wares fetched in European markets (granted, people were hungry), U.S. farmers grew too much wheat, barley, and cotton. The surplus caused prices to drop and stripped agronomists of the means to pay loans for equipment and land. They organized and began lobbying Congress—hard. By early 1929, the American Farm Bureau Federation had proposed steep tariffs on Argentine corn, Philippine coconut oil, Cuban sugar, and some three to four hundred other imported items.

Until then, food manufacturers had been considered part of the agricultural sector. But as Eastern and Western legislators bickered over raising percentage points on the foreign competitors of their home state industries (manufacturing or agriculture, respectively), they based their argument on the fact that the other sector was bigger and more prosperous. To better portray agriculture as the weakling in the tussle, the head of the Farm Bureau Federation gave "processed food items" a quickie divorce, moving them to the industrial side of the ledger, where they have stayed ever since. The Smoot-Hawley Tariff—laden with rate increases on 22,000–23,000 farm and factory goods, according to the 1930 Congressional Record—waddled into law on June 17, 1930. World trade immediately plummeted, and the Great Depression settled down to stay.

The term "processed food" has polarized people ever since. It is ridiculously inclusive by design. Like most polemic phrases, it wasn't coined for accuracy, but for breadth—to maximize its impact when weaponized. Thus, to have a rational conversation about this category of sustenance, we need to be more precise. Can we identify the 40,000–50,000 items available for sale in the typical super-market, develop a classification system most of us can agree upon, and use it to make meaningful judgments about our food purchases? Luckily for us, the answer is yes.

It turns out that the vagueness that makes it hard for reg-ular people to define processed food also flummoxes health researchers. In 2011, Jennifer M. Poti, then a nutritional epidemiology doctoral candidate at the University of North Carolina at Chapel Hill, was looking for a way to assess how much processed food children eat and if it could be contrib-uting to high rates of juvenile obesity. Surprisingly, she found there was no clarity or consensus in the literature. "Lack of clear definition for processed foods hinders our ability to quantify their contribution to u.s. diet," she titles one section of her 2014 thesis, "Development of a Novel Classification System to Determine the Role of Processed and Convenience Foods in the Diets of u.s. Households." "A primary reason for this gap in the research literature is the lack of clear, comprehensive, and universally accepted definition of processed foods."

Poti then proposed a new system, based on both degree of processing and level of convenience. Neither of these is perfect. The processing spectrum ranges from minimally processed, moderately processed, processed, and ultra-processed. However, there is disagreement about where to put such well-established techniques as "canning, freezing, preparation of mixtures and seasoning." Even further from perfection is that the classification system reveals a fair amount of ignorance about what really happens during food processing. As is true for consumers as a whole, Poti expresses greatest concern about additives, including our ancient preservatives, sugar and salt, and the alteration of food from its original state. Unfortunately, this completely ignores the bulk of what happens throughout modern industrial food-making, which employs machines that apply mechanics, temperature, pressure, and old and new kinds of radiant energy; uses additives that leave no trace and aren't listed on labels; and has a panoply of science-derived tools to manipulate ingredients at the molecular level. It also completely misunderstands the high level of processing in what are viewed as wholesome staples. Consider, for example: milk (pasteurization, homogenization), yogurt (thermalization, low and high temperature pasteurization, ultra-heat treatment, sterilization, and, frequently, the addition of agents such as inulin for a creamier texture), cheese (don't get scared, but add into the dairy mix microfiltration to separate proteins and encapsulated exogenous liposomes to accelerate ripening), and supermarket bread (do you really want to go there?). However, for now, let's accept Poti's categories as a starting place.

The convenience scale has similar issues. It considers convenient ready-to-eat foods and prepared or heat-and-serve meals, but inconvenient such products as boxed mac 'n' cheese or cake mixes that require a small amount of additional work by the consumer. Really? Is it that hard to boil a pot of water for pasta, tear open a cheese packet, and add a pat of butter and a dollop of milk? Or in the case of cake mix, add water, vegetable oil, and eggs, beat the mixture, and pour it into a greased pan?

Poti and her colleagues classified more than 1.2 million items! Based on her system, they analyzed food and beverage purchases for 157,142 families between 2000 and 2012. What they found: "Over ¾ of calories purchased by u.s. households came from processed (15.9 percent) and ultra-processed (61 percent) foods and beverages in 2012 (939 kcal/d per capita). By convenience, ready-to-eat (68.1 percent) and ready-to-heat (15.2 percent) products supplied the majority of household calories, with a significant upward trend in ready-to-heat foods between 2000 and 2012." Canadians and the British don't fare much better; 61.7 percent of the calories in the Canadian diet and 63.4 percent in the United Kingdom come from processed foods, according to studies with similar classification systems done there. Poti and her collaborators warned that "many more ultra-processed foods, 60.4 percent, exceed recommended daily maximums for saturated fat, sugar, and salt than for ready-to-eat food (27.1 percent), less-processed foods (5.6 percent), or foods requiring cooking, 4.9 percent." In a nutshell—people are eating a lot of these items. Let's take a careful look at what each category contains, add some distinctions of our own, and use common sense to weigh each foodstuff's pros and cons. If it seems as though it could be eaten or drunk as part of a reasonably healthy diet, we may be able to reclaim large swathes of the supermarket from the food nags.

Categorization of Food by Level of Processing

Minimally Processed

Single-ingredient foods and beverages with little to no processing. The food is similar to as found raw or in nature, although may have a part removed, such as skinless, boneless chicken parts or skim milk. Examples include milk (biting my tongue about pasteurization, homogenization, centrifugal separation of fats, ultrafiltration to remove proteins and calcium molecules, reverse osmosis and ultra osmosis, all of which are used to create a safe, long-lasting, consistent product with the exact combination of fat, protein, and lactose preferred by the consumer), eggs, meat, fruits, and vegetables.

Moderately Processed

This category covers ingredients such as sugar, oil, and flour, which have undergone chemical or mechanical treatment, but are still recognizable. It also includes foods that have been preserved or somehow prepared for cooking, such as canned goods, milled flour, fruit juice concentrates, and yogurt.

Processed

Again, there are two subcategories here. The first are minimally and moderately processed foods to which some ingredients have been added to enhance the flavor but not to change its properties, such as salted nuts and canned fruits and vegetables. Processed whole-grain products—breads, crackers, cereals, and so on—are also included in this group.

Ultra-processed

These are "multi-component mixtures of combined ingredients, processed to the extent that they no longer resemble their basic component foods as found in nature in unprocessed form." Within this classification, there are two branches: condiments and additions, such as ketchup, margarine, and jarred sauces. And then everything else: white bread, soda, cookies, salty snacks, candy, and pre-prepared mixed dishes (I'm not sure what this refers to—perhaps TV dinners?).

Unfortunately, Poti's elaborate system is built on a shaky understanding of what food processing actually is. Thus, her vision tends to make meaningless distinctions between items such as frozen vegetables without and with salt (granted, important if you have very high blood pressure or Ménière's disease, but not a huge concern for the rest of us), categorizing one as moderately processed and the other as processed. Truly? The addition of a bit of sodium chloride changes the nature of the food so much? A bit of sugar? At the same time, it ignores, presumably for lack of knowledge, the numerous other techniques that are used to modify industrial food. But it's the best we've got, so to eliminate this minor difference and reduce redundancy, I'm going to conflate the "moderately processed" and "processed categories" in the table found below.

The other dimension Poti considers is convenience. There are three categories, reflecting how much work people have to do before eating the item.

Categorization of Food by Level of Convenience

Inconvenient

Foods and beverages that require preparation before being consumed. This can range from cooking raw meats, eggs, potatoes, and dried beans; chopping fruits and vegetables; baking; boiling pasta; and cooking and assembling partially prepared foods such as boxed mixes and macaroni and cheese.

Convenient

This category requires minimal preparation and consumer culinary skill. It consists mainly of ready-to-heat items or frozen foods that only call for defrosting—if that—such as "frozen dinners or pizza, frozen waffles, canned soup, hot dogs, instant oatmeal, canned or frozen vegetables, and powdered drink mixes."

Highly Convenient

Open mouth, insert food. This category includes anything you can eat without any preparation whatsoever. In addition to the bakery items, savory snacks, and canned or bottled drinks, it also includes fresh items such as fruit, baby carrots, and bagged salad.

I've unified the two scales in a table where a food can be placed both according to its level of processing and its level of convenience. Within each category, I've also split foods into two types, which I think help us to clarify what are probably acceptable additions to our diet and what should be used sparingly: meal or snack, beverage or dessert. As we shall see, there are many perfectly healthy, highly processed foods. It is only when they fall into the snack category that they become sugar, fat, and sodium weapons of mass destruction. That category includes such perennial crowd-pleasers as alcohol; candy; energy drinks; cookies, cake, pie, and pastries; ice cream; crackers, pretzels, tortilla chips, and cheese puffs; soda; and whipped topping. I think we can all agree that these items should be enjoyed in small quantities.

The early twenty-first century has been a period of deep division in the United States and elsewhere. And I'm not talking about politics, partisan though they are. To the indignation of many followers of the traditional meat-based American and British diets, vegetarianism's militant vanguard, veganism, has won many new converts. Some have made the change to avoid taking animal lives. Others to live sustainably or more healthfully. Most often, it's a combination of all three. Whatever the reason, this market segment, which includes many millennials, has food manufacturers salivating.

Companies large and small have stepped into the breach. They sex up old standbys by replacing such functional

	Inconvenient Requires cooking or preparation	Convenient Ready to heat	Highly Convenient Ready to eat
COMMON FOOD ITEMS BY BOTH LEVEL OF PROCESSING AND CONVENIENCE			
Minimally Processed	Meal: Brewed coffee; brewed tea; dried beans; eggs; some fresh fruits or vegetables; fresh meat, sausage, or bacon; whole cereals such as oatmeal; whole grains such as brown rice; whipping cream	Meal: Frozen fruits, vegetables, or meats with nothing added	Meal: Condiments such as honey, herbs, and spices Snack, (caloric) beverage or dessert: Dried fruits and nuts; fresh fruits and some vegetables; milk
Processed	Meal: Canned tomatoes; flavored oil; flour; maple syrup; oil; pasta; frozen and/or seasoned meat; seasoning salts; smoked or cured bacon, ham, or seafood; sugar; white and instant rice	Meal: Butter; canned fruits, vegetables, beans, and fish or meats with salt, sugar, or other additives; frozen French fries; instant coffee; refrigerated or frozen vegetables; sour cream; sweetened/flavored hot cereal Snack, beverage, or dessert: Cocoa mix; dry milk; flavored popcorn (microwaveable or pre-popped); frozen juice concentrate	Meal: Whole-grain bread, tortillas, and bagels Snack, beverage, or dessert: Cheese; chocolate milk; crackers; evaporated milk; fruit juice; jam; nuts with salt or oil; peanut butter; potato chips; refrigerated, pre-cut fruit; RTE cereals with whole grains; soy milk; sweetened condensed milk; whipped cream; yogurt; crackers

| Highly Processed | Meal: Baking chocolate; bread crumbs/breading with refined grains or added sugar/fat; boxed mac 'n' cheese and other prepared pasta or rice dishes; pancake or waffle mixes; pudding mixes | Meal: Alfredo sauce, barbecue sauce; bouillon; canned or boxed broth, icing; canned baked beans; frozen onion rings; frozen or canned pasta dishes (lasagna, ravioli, spaghetti, and meatballs); frozen pizza; frozen vegetables in sauce; marinades, and other condiments; hot dogs; instant rice/pasta dish mixes; noodle- or rice-based soups; meat-based frozen meals (Salisbury steak, breaded meat, chicken, nuggets, fish sticks); pasta- or rice-based frozen meals; RTH grain-based dishes (burritos, sandwiches, pot pies); RTH meat dishes (meat loaf, crab cakes, buffalo wings, pot roast, bar-becue); RTH pancakes, waffles, or biscuits; sauce/seasoning mixes; sausage; tater tots, hash brown patties, re-formed French fries, RTH or instant potato dishes (mashed potatoes, stuffed baked potatoes); tomato sauce

Snack, beverage, or dessert: Powdered beverage mixes | Meal: Artificial sweetener; bread, tortillas, rolls, or bagels; entrée garden salads; flavored water; frozen or canned pasta dishes (lasagna, ravioli, spaghetti, and meatballs); frozen pizza; instant rice/pasta dish mixes; ketchup; margarine; mayonnaise; meat-based soups; noodle or rice-based soups; pancake syrup; pasta or rice-based frozen meals; pressed/formed lunchmeats (bologna, salami, some turkey) or ham; RTE breakfast cereals with refined grains; RTE grain-based dishes (burritos, sandwiches, pot pies); RTE potato salad; salad dressing; shortening; Spam; stuffing mix; vegetable-based soups

Snack, (caloric) beverage or dessert: Alcohol; candy; cheese dip/queso; cheese-cake; chocolate; chocolate or yogurt-covered dried fruit or nuts; coffee bever-ages; creamer; dairy-based chip/veggie dip; energy drinks; frozen yogurt; fruit drinks; fruit snacks; gelatin fruit salads; grain-based desserts (cookies, cake, pie, pastries); hummus; ice cream; jelly; popsicles; pro-cessed cheese; restructured potato chips; RTE gelatin; RTE pudding; salsa; salty snacks (crackers, pretzels, tortilla chips, cheese puffs); soda; sorbet; sports drinks; whipped topping |

ingredients as cattle bone char (bleaches cane sugar), ruminant-stomach rennet (solidifies milk protein to make cheese), and texture-imparting gelatin from animal skin and bones with plant-based alternatives. They have also come up with a plethora of meat substitutes that go far beyond old-school tofu, tempeh, and seitan, the most notable examples of which—Gardein tenders, Quorn patties, and Beyond Meat and Impossible burgers—are bringing vegetarians back to supermarket freezers and fast-food restaurants in droves. Lost in this flesh-free bonanza is the fact that many of these foods are highly processed and, as such, should trigger their own set of concerns from the food conscious. Vegan foods don't stint on the methylcellulose and xanthan gum. And hexane, a neurotoxin, is used to create textured vegetable protein, soy isolates, and hydrolyzed protein. (It should be noted that these three are also used in many nonvegan foods for functional reasons and to add protein and essential amino acids.)

It's time to stop making processed food a double bogey-man, first, as an easy out for the anxiety most consumers feel about not understanding the exacting science and technology that goes into creating everything from bottled fruit juice and packaged deli meat to shelf-stable tortillas and bricks of supermarket cheddar. And second, as the culprit for the uncontained spread of the Global North's midriff. The term was invented for a food fight; to neutralize its pejorative association, we must understand—and define—it better. How is the food made? What are the raw and other ingredients? What are the processing techniques? And is it eaten as part of a meal or as a snack, drink, or dessert?

Rather than categorically excluding processed food, let's identify which subsets of it can be eaten regularly as part of a relatively healthy diet and which should be saved for occasional treats—and then act accordingly. My proposal: Monitor your intake of highly processed, highly convenient snacks, beverages, and desserts (the section in italics in the table). For everything else, stop worrying! As long as you eat a well-balanced diet that includes plenty of fruits and vegetables (fresh, canned, or frozen) and avoid sugary drinks, whether soda or juice, you'll be fine.

2

HISTORY OF PROCESSED FOOD AND TWENTY-FIRST-CENTURY INNOVATIONS

When I was little and visiting my maternal grandfather, who'd grown up in the Connecticut River Valley wedged between southern New Hampshire and Vermont, I loved to read a burlap-covered scrapbook his older sister Elsie had made. Inside were numerous anecdotes from his life, drawn and told in black India ink. My favorite depicted Gagoo plunged face first into a barrel, legs waving in the air. "Lester falls into the cracker barrel," was the caption. It's incredible to think that a little over one hundred years ago, barrels or tins full of common crackers, a floury New England favorite that lasted forever and went with everything (to his dying day, my grandfather liked them crumbled into milk), was one of the few processed foods in the household pantry.

Manufactured edibles first appeared in the nineteenth century with canned goods, cracker barrels, and the occasional condiment, an era when mushrooming urban populations made transforming cheap, perishable raw materials into long-lasting prepared items a profitable proposition. Although the term "processed food" itself was coined in the very late 1920s, the category only gathered steam after the Second World War, which, with its rapacious hunger for rations that could be shipped around the globe and stored for months or years, forever altered the American food system. From 1941 to 1945, local and regional companies got the sales boost they needed to go national. The field of food science—led by the army—was practically invented, and a countrywide system of university and industry labs put into place. Stringent military requirements forced consumer goods companies to develop scientifically based formulations, or industrial recipes, often using new chemical compounds or processes developed by the armed forces and their collaborators, and favored bland, universally appealing products over more strongly flavored and ethnic ones. Most of these items depended on tried-and-true technologies, invented in the first quarter of the twentieth century or before. Campbell's chicken soup, which first went on sale in 1934, relies on canning, invented in 1809 by Frenchman Nicolas Appert. Finger-staining, orange Cheetos appeared in 1948 and are a delectable cross between 1930s cereal extruders and Second World War-era dehydrated cheese powder. Swanson's iconic roast turkey TV dinner, which hit the supermarket aisles in 1954, was the progeny of Clarence Birdseye's 1920s discovery of quick-freezing.

The postwar decades saw huge growth in all kinds of food additives—an estimated 25,000 chemical compounds were tested between 1940 and 1960. Soon after the 1958 Food and Additives Act was enacted to regulate them, some 2,000 had already been approved as Generally Recognized as Safe (GRAS; there are now 9,000). These included compounds in most of the categories that exist today—antimicrobials, antioxidants, artificial colors, artificial flavors, flavor enhancers, emulsifiers, stabilizers, thickeners, humectants, anti-caking agents, and plasticizers, among others. In combination with engineering breakthroughs from ultra-high temperature processing, flash-freezing, freeze-dehydration, radiation sterilization, and aseptic processing, as well as better packaging, the number of processed foods exploded in the second half of the twentieth century. The American—and international—kitchen hasn't been the same since.

At first, the new convenience items were heralded as progress. A 1955 *Women's Day* magazine cover shows a tow-headed mother, father, and daughter lolling in the blue surf with a headline promising "more time for fun" with their "cook-less cookbook." The following year, the head of the Food and Drug Administration (FDA) exulted "that the housewife of the future will practice the art of cooking only occasionally as hobby." Today, American and other Global North women—and, yes, this is still overwhelmingly a feminine duty—spend less time than ever before shopping, cooking, and cleaning up after meals, an average of just one hour and twenty minutes. But rather than celebrating this newfound liberty from antiquity's most unremitting household chore, we've reversed course. Instead, the mother who relies on industrial food to feed her family is chastised.

Our optimism about processed food darkened to skepticism and then pessimism in the 1970s, following the births of the environmental and consumer protection movements and culminating with the publication of Ralph Nader's polemic, *Chemical Feast*. It was all too accurate (at the time), and slowly gave rise to a foodie countermovement which wove together concerns about health, the planet, and late-stage capitalism with gourmandism, a trend perfectly embodied by Michael Pollan in *The Omnivore's Dilemma*. A central tenet was not only to reject this class of nourishment, but to view it with deep distrust. Like the tobacco industry, which was buffeted by decades of well-deserved attacks for selling harmful products and obfuscating the damage they did to human beings, large food companies are indicted as nefarious peddlers of addictive substances that compel us to polish off thousands of calories at a single sitting.

As a child, I toured both a potato chip factory and an ice-cream manufacturing facility, where I watched, mesmerized, as waterfalls of chips poured from the fryer and huge lagoons of cream and sugar swirled. (Not to mention every child's dream: unlimited samples!) Later, when I worked at the Harvard Business School after college, I visited a chicken-packing plant for a project on labor-management relations; conveyor belts twisted back and forth from wall to ceiling and over the blood-stained floor, whisking plucked carcasses by blade-wielding Mexican immigrants. Yet despite these experiences, I found it very hard to understand the science and technology that goes into turning raw agricultural goods into finished food products. Instilled by labels featuring small, family farms and steaming, home-cooked meals, I pictured it as something akin to what I did in my own kitchen, just on a bigger scale. That packaged, sliced turkey breast? Surely somewhere immaculate, white-aproned workers were sliding dozens of glistening, golden birds out of gigantic ovens, carving off the breasts and passing them through slicers, after which they'd be sealed into packages. How quaint and how wrong.

Food manufacturing often bears no resemblance to what people do at home—in ingredients, in chronology, in tools, and in techniques. Take, for example, the aforementioned sliced turkey breast, an item my middle daughter never fails to demand when I go to the store. The highest-end variety, the kind the in-store deli attendant shaves to your specifications, is truly composed of turkey breasts. But that's where the similarity with your T-Day repast ends. These are brined for days, needled full of spices, squeezed between two heavy rollers to break down cartilage and gristle, tumbled and massaged to release a sticky exudate that binds them together and finally boiled, steamed, baked, or smoked in porous plastic, often for hours on end. They are then removed from the first wrapper, quickly fried in oil to impart a brown finish, and wrapped in plastic again.

The cheaper variety, which comes straight from the factory to your grocery cart in its own package, veers even further from how we make turkey at home. Breast meat and 'other white meat' are extracted from pockets all over the bird and then the disintegrated muscle filaments are combined into a slurry, a runny paste, with salt, water and sodium phosphate for juiciness, sodium nitrates for curing, and sodium erythorbate for imparting an appetizing hue. After the log is cooked, it is sliced, inserted into a package, and then flushed with gases to extend shelf life and retard microbial growth, a higher risk because of the greater surface area of the sliced meats. However, both these cold-cut processes are now old-fashioned.

In the past three decades, the modern supermarket has been remade—largely by revolutionary new processing techniques that cater to the public's desire for more natural edibles. Supermarket perimeters, where perishables are found, have expanded; spending there is up almost 5 percent since 1992, according to Progressive Grocery's (PGA) Annual Consumer Expenditure Study. We're eating more fresh things—since the 1960s, the number of fruits and vegetables in the produce section has doubled, from 170 to 340, according to the Food Marketing Institute. Many now come packaged, immaculately clean, and cut into bite-sized pieces; consumption of them is up from 7.6 percent of grocery spending in the 1960s to 11.6 today, according to the Food Marketing Institute. And we're also eating more minimally processed, prepared items, thanks to next generation, "cold" processing techniques that allow manufacturers to achieve longer shelf life without chemical additives while conserving the taste, texture, and nutrients of fresh foods.

Relatedly, purchases in supermarket flyover territory—the center aisles, typically lined with various types of shelf-stable food in plastic, cardboard, glass, or metal containers—has declined from 53.4 to 46.3 percent since 1992, again according to PGA. But even in the supermarket hinterlands, a sea change is afoot. Industrial enzymes fill in for many synthetic processing aids, while plant-based additives are slashing polysyllabic words from the ingredient list. In fact, since 1998, about three-quarters of the six hundred Food and Drug Administration's (FDA) GRAS notices have been for substances derived from microbes, plants, or animals. These new foods may eliminate the most important objection to convenience items: healthfulness.

"Clean label" is the industry catchphrase for packaged foods that contain few or no chemical additives, list only recognizable ingredients, and are minimally processed. A steady drumbeat of major conglomerates such as Kellogg's, Campbell's, Nestlé, and Kraft Heinz have announced rejiggered recipes for their flagship cereals, soups, candies and snacks, and convenience foods. Less sugar and salt. No artificial flavors, colors, or preservatives. Food system and public health activists have applauded the development. But few or none have asked how manufacturers can suddenly abandon formulations that, for decades, allowed these foods to last virtually forever without deteriorating or becoming unsafe. And the food industry, accustomed to media attacks and consumer suspicion, rather than publicizing these changes, has hunkered down, introducing their "New Selects" and "Natural Choice" lines with no explanation of how the improvements are achieved.

What's to hide? Most people would probably be relieved to discover the real way these ready-to-eat and heat-and-serve foods stay good for weeks or even months. Because what lies behind the clean label is a lot of spanking new science and technology, most of which truly seems to lead to healthier food. Below is a guide to some of the standouts from new twenty-first-century food-processing techniques.

Cold Processing

Since the time of Napoleon, heat sterilization has been the gold standard for safe food preservation. Unfortunately, the high temperature and long cooking, in addition to eliminating harmful microorganisms, often destroys flavor, texture, and vitamins—compare just-made to canned tuna or green beans. In the 1990s and early 2000s, the u.s. military spearheaded research on a whole suite of techniques that didn't use heat or used very little to cook and conserve food. Among the treatments, used alone or in tandem, were those that employ high pressure, electromagnetic energy, and chemical state changes. A few have been successfully commercialized, and several more have the potential to be. These nonthermal or cold processing techniques maintain all the attributes of fresh food without chemical additives and far less salt and sugar. Early research on their health impacts has found they leave few or no residual chemical reaction products in the food.

If you dip your tortilla chips into packaged guacamole; quench your thirst with a bottle of raw apple, celery, kale, and collard juice; or stuff your sandwiches with preservative-free pastrami, then you've consumed foods made with high-pressure processing (HPP). The method works by placing food surrounded by water inside a heavy-duty vessel, then upping the pressure to around 60,000 psi, about 4,000 times that of a stovetop pressure cooker, for between 5 and 10 minutes. The water compresses somewhat, but mostly holds its volume, thus transmitting the tremendous force to the food without crushing it. Some of the bonds holding together large, life-critical molecules such as lipids and proteins are broken, killing any living organisms. But since little heat is generated and the treatment is brief, fruits, vegetables, juices, and meats look and taste barely cooked.

"Of the [nonthermal] technologies . . . HPP is the most commercially accepted. When used for in-container pasteurization of foods and beverages, it is enjoying increasing use, particularly for so-called clean label products—those without the types of preservatives traditionally used in the food industry," says Kevin Higgins, managing editor of *Food Processing* magazine.

A second nonthermal technique that has made inroads at the supermarket is pulsed electric fields (PEF). This is the application of up to 80 kW/cm of power—about as much as is produced by a large home generator—in incredibly short (think one-millionth of a second) but repeated bursts to the food. The strong charge produces tiny pores in cell membranes, causing the cytoplasm to leak out and surrounding fluid to penetrate, fatal to any bacteria or fungi in the food. Like HPP, PEF is used to pasteurize juices, as well as for other "pumpables" such as soup, milk, and yogurt drinks. It also helps extract oils, sugars, and other substances from tissue and assists in dehydration and preparation of French fries, frozen and chilled potato products, and chips. In fact, according to Gustavo Barbosa-Cánovas, director of the Washington State University Center for Non-Thermal Processing of Food and one of the key people behind the development of the technology, "[at Pulsemaster], the largest company processing potatoes, all the machinery to do the tissue conditioning for drying, all the machines are based on PEF."

In addition, ultraviolet light and ultrasound are often used, although Barbosa-Cánovas cautions that "all the processes are either pasteurization or decontamination, not sterilization," so they must be refrigerated or used in tandem with other preservation methods, including some heat.

Ultraviolet light, which induces fatal genetic mutations in the DNA of any lurking bacteria or viruses, requires a transparent package for the rays to pass through, so is applied primarily to disinfect water, juices, and as a surface decontaminant for meats, fruits, and vegetables. Ultrasound creates tiny bubbles that disrupt cellular function; in combination with high temperature, it can homogenize and extend the shelf life of milk. It also helps cheeses such as *queso fresco* retain liquid, augmenting their yield and therefore their profitability.

More new technologies are in the pipeline. Microwave-assisted thermal sterilization (MATS) uses a small amount of cooking plus microwaves to kill microorganisms. It's being commercialized by 915 Labs, an equipment company, which says that eventually its partners will be selling full meals, akin to a TV dinner, that can be stored at room temperature. Another technique combines a vacuum with microwave drying; it can suck most of the moisture from fresh fruits and vegetables, which leaves them shrunken, but still crisp and crunchy. The army plans to use this technique to provide miniaturized produce as part of combat rations. And cold plasma electrifies a gas so that it forms highly reactive molecules that lethally damage microbes. Barbosa-Cánovas says that although this technology is in its infancy, it looks very promising as a way to decontaminate herbs and spices, which, since they are often imported from countries with less robust food safety systems, may harbor dangerous pathogens. (Most are currently irradiated.)

Industrial Enzymes

Few people would guess modern packaged food's most ubiquitous ingredient. Except in the produce and meat departments, "most everywhere else you go in the grocery market, an [industrial] enzyme has been involved as a processing aid in that food," says John Sedivy, recently director of business development at Novozymes and chair of the Enzyme Technical Association, a trade group. Enzymes, proteins found in all living creatures that speed up one specific chemical reaction by a factor of millions or even billions, have a long tradition in food preparation. Naturally occurring chymosin in rennet, from calves' stomachs, is responsible for curdling cheese; amylase, found in wheat, yeast, and barley, for making bread rise and beer bubble; and trypsin from animal poop, for softening leather. (OK, not a food, but still!)

Commercial enzymes have been sold since the beginning of the twentieth century and those for food since the 1930s, when scientists first learned how to culture them and separate them from their host organism, typically a fungi or bacteria. But the present-day market didn't develop until the early 1990s when microfiltration (films with tiny holes that act as microscopic sieves), cell immobilization, and genetic engineering technologies became less expensive and easier to use. Today the biological structures, most commonly bred industrially by fungi, often replace chemical additives in food, as well as offer other applications, such as keeping bread from staling, tenderizing meat, and extracting cooking oil. In 2020, the global market for food enzymes was more than $2.9 billion, according to an analysis by Global Market Insights.

Sedivy isn't kidding when he says enzymes can be found everywhere. Manufacturers use industrial lipases to break down fats and oils, making them more stable, improving mixing, and ridding them of trans-fats. Proteases, which alter proteins, are common in all sorts of dairy products, from cheeses and yogurt to lactose-free milk, and in meats where they are used to tenderize, create broth, and add umami flavor. The bakery and snack section are chock-full of carbohydrate-loving enzymes, which break down starch for yeast and prevent staling, as well as gluten snackers that keep dough stable during rising. They're used to reduce the pulping of coffee beans from over thirty to just four hours and to control oxygen in packaging to maintain freshness. And finally, they're instrumental in making the much-vilified high-fructose corn syrup.

Unlike chemical additives, which frequently persist in the finished product and thus must be listed as an ingredient, enzymes are usually inactivated by processing and disappear into the food. "Enzymes work very quickly. They work under very specific conditions. You have to have the right range of pH, the right range of temperature and, in addition, the right substrate or food stock, and then they work," explains Sedivy. "If those conditions aren't there, they don't do anything. And once they do their thing, they basically denature, so they're no longer viable. They are pieces of protein." To date, there have been no known adverse effects found with consuming them; the only negative health impacts have been inhalation allergies in workers brought on by mishandling or improper manufacturing conditions.

Plant-Based Additives

The third major trend behind clean label is the one shoppers are most likely to observe and understand, new additives and functional ingredients derived from plants. These are replacing synthetic colors, flavors, and preservatives, as well as stabilizers, thickeners, and emulsifiers. It is also the one that, paradoxically, poses most difficulties for food businesses, which, as they comply with the public's demand for natural ingredients, must cope with a plethora of complications that come from using a less stable, more costly, and less consistent substitute.

"For example, if you're going to use natural color paprika and turmeric, it doesn't last as long, especially if you're using glass containers," says Claudia Dziuk O'Donnell, who organizes the Clean Label Conference, an annual event running for more than a decade. A work-around for manmade flavors is to simply use a larger quantity of key ingredients, a fix that should make consumers happy. Dziuk O'Donnell cites the example of monosodium glutamate (MSG), an amino acid that is typically created by fermenting corn, sugar, or tapioca. To replicate its savory punch, food manufacturers are "looking at using more of the natural ingredients. Mushrooms? Parmesan? Tomatoes? It may be more expensive and not quite as consistent, but it does say Parmesan and not MSG [on the label] . . . And the end result will be more nutritious." Rosemary and clove essential oils take the place of chemical bacteriocins and antifungals, and starches and fibers from sources such as sweet potatoes, chia seeds, and the South American quillaja tree are being used instead of modified cornstarch, xanthan gum, and lecithin.

* * * * *

It's time we revisited processed food, which has provided us with safe, abundant, convenient, and inexpensive nourishment for more than a century. For obvious reasons, you might not want to subsist solely on Chef Boyardee and Ring Dings and, indeed, there's ample medical research to support this decision. But if you look elsewhere in the grocery store—and, please, avert your eyes from the soda and snacks which, like all vices, should be enjoyed in moderation—you'll find many products that already meet your demand for real ingredients, less salt and sugar, and few or no scary-sounding chemicals. Putting dinner on the table need no longer be a choice between your time and your health. If you find chopping therapeutic and reading recipes relaxing, by all means, do it. But for everyone else, there's take-out. And meal kits. And, yes, processed food.

3

AN AGE-OLD TIME SUCK: WOMEN AND COOKING

Commuter traffic roared on the major highway that runs behind Ceci's house in Somerville, Massachusetts. I parked and texted, "We're here!" Ceci texted back, "Not ready yet. Sorry! Come on up." I suppressed a wave of irritation. Many people in our multi-town, home-educators group made financial sacrifices so one parent could be full time with the children, and I'd gotten in the habit of giving rides to those without cars or whose partners needed their only vehicle. But it was common courtesy to be ready to go, especially since this morning's activity, a walk in the Middlesex Fells, was led by a naturalist who was as punctual as he was knowledgeable. Sighing, I told Gabriela, nine years old, and Mariela, seven, to unbuckle their seatbelts. They scrambled out and onto the porch, where there were several trashcans and a huge pile of slightly discolored plastic toys—bicycles, tricycles, assorted balls, pails, and shovels. I rang the bell and Ceci buzzed us in.

Not ready yet was an understatement. Ceci had the baby, dressed in a disposable diaper, in a highchair and was trying to spoon baby food into his closed mouth. His arms windmilled in excitement as his eyes darted around the small apartment, following his siblings as they chased each other. A boy with striking eyes and loose black curls and a girl with a cascade of hair to her waist called to my kids to come play. I clenched my teeth. Boot, who combined identifying flora with reciting poetry, would leave and we'd miss the hike entirely. But one look at the beseeching expression on Ceci's narrow face dissolved my annoyance. "Can I help you?"

"Yes. Can you give the older ones some breakfast?" She gestured to an economy-sized package of single-serving General Mills cereals that seemed to be a medley of its sugariest hits. I corralled the children, took orders, and handed out boxes of Cocoa Puffs, Cinnamon Toast Crunch, and Lucky Charms. "Milk?" Ceci looked at me, wincing, her almond-shaped brown eyes tired; I noticed the gray strand in her long, black hair. She shook her head. "I know it's not very healthy, but it's all I have, and I don't have time to make a hot breakfast." She thought I was judging her. I felt terrible. Later, when we'd finally loaded all six children in the car and the steady bedlam masked our conversation, she confided in me that her short-fused husband had exploded in anger the night before and she'd asked him to leave. Foodies, when you call for whole foods, home cooking, and family dinners, your wagging fingers and scolding tongues are an implicit criticism of women like Ceci, casting shame upon how she has chosen to spend her two scantest resources, time and money.

A woman's obligation to nourish her family is a universal norm, and the rare rebel faces harsher censure than if she had committed grand larceny. On Friday nights, after the work week is finally done, Rafael and I like to stream a movie on our large, flat-screen TV. We're not big fans of Hollywood, instead preferring the small, real-life dramas of foreign and independent titles. No matter the film's origin, there's an evitable scene I brace for. In the 2017 American hit *Lady Bird*, Marion scrambles eggs for her recalcitrant teenage daughter. In the 2016 Japanese drama *Harmonium*, Akié leaps up from the table to get seconds for her husband and his ex-con friend, Yasaka. In the 2016 French movie *Things to Come* (*L'Avenir*), Isabelle Huppert's character, a former communist and well-respected philosophy professor, serves dinner to her seated husband and son. These moments are so insignificant that the action and dialogue of the films continue without a ripple. But I notice and wonder about it every time. Why is food preparation still mostly women's work? And what does that mean for our lives?

To truly understand, we must go back in time to before humans diverged from the rest of the primate branch of the evolutionary tree. Most monkeys and their tailless cousins, the apes, or hominoids, are hooked on sugar. Primarily frugivores, they munch fruit all day, although the wild versions of these are a lot less luscious than the specimens found in the modern supermarket. Each simian forages for its own swollen plant ova, periodically supplemented with a flora or fauna protein. Depending on their preferred secondary food, monkeys and apes have two basic types of digestive systems. Those who enjoy a good grasshopper, grub, bird, egg, or rodent have a simple stomach and colon, with the major action taking place in the relatively long small intestine, where enzymes break down proteins, fats, and sugars. Those who must stuff themselves silly with leaves have a large and complicated stomach and colon system, characterized by a voluminous large intestine in which plant cellulose is fermented to extract its nutrients. Only three primates— chimpanzees, baboons, and humans—are true omnivores, easily switching among fruit, seeds, leaves, and animal matter.

But the human gut has a further difference from our Great Ape siblings. Our small intestines are very long—more than 19½ feet (6 m)—and our large intestines, where fermentation of cellulose happens, quite short, around 5 feet (1.5 m). This more compact digestive system appeared, along with smaller teeth and bigger brains, with the emergence of *Homo erectus*, our grandparent species, in Africa 1.8 million years ago. Why? We'd found a way to make food softer; more digestible; more nutrient-dense; and, if it is scavenged, bacteria-free, liberating us from the daylong mastication sessions that keep other mammals and primates occupied. Cooking!

Primate food processing was nothing new—and under-taken by both sexes. Chimpanzees will crack open nuts by smashing them between a rock and a club. Old World species from Asia, Africa, and Europe often have cheek pouches where they store seeds and allow salivary enzymes to extract nutrients. Monkeys and apes also remove spines and thorns from plants, poke insects out of logs with sticks, wash their food, and position and tear leaves with their hands. And some species, such as chimpanzees and bonobos, hunt, although more often solo than in groups. While this activity is dominated by males, females also participate. (Recent studies suggest that, in fact, female chimpanzees are the ones most likely to use implements in slaughter.)

Thermal processing, using heat to prepare food, was different. It took time, know-how, and the willingness to stay put. Which meant that whoever took on KP duty (or kitchen patrol, a joking military term) would have to skip prolonged hunting expeditions, especially if, as some scientists think, these were simply running down prey until it, exhausted, collapsed onto the ground. These restrictions were well suited to women of childbearing years, who could be heavily pregnant, nursing, or carrying little ones. Thus began the mommy track. The practice overturned the typical primate feeding *modus operandi* of every monkey for itself, except for mothers and young and very occasional sharing between adults. One or several *Homo erectus* females could prepare batches of food, which could be eaten collectively. "[C]ooking has made possible one of the most distinctive features of human society: the modern form of the sexual division of labor," says anthropologist Richard Wrangham in his 2009 book *Catching Fire: How Cooking Made Us Human*. Dinner is, quite literally, the foundation of the patriarchy.

Old habits die hard. After almost two million years of daily practice, the combined forces of the industrial, agricultural, and sexual revolutions have done little to shake loose the primeval association of women and nourishment. Today, women around the world are still responsible for family food preparation. Of course, making group meals is just one of a host of gender-based household duties, albeit the one that takes the most time.

Aware of housework's impact on women's lives, a few years ago I came up with a scheme to introduce a more equitable allocation of responsibilities in my own home. I stuck four lined Post-it notes on the refrigerator. "Please write down the chores you do. At the end of the week, we'll figure out if anything needs to change." I recorded my contributions zealously: cooking, dishes, laundry, sweeping, swiping (bathrooms). Although they did a couple household tasks—a load of dishes here, take out the trash there—my husband and daughters declined to participate. At the end of the week, I sighed and removed my overflowing list and the three blank notes alongside it. Perhaps they forgot. But I suspect my family didn't want to recognize who does and who doesn't benefit from our existing arrangement.

As it happens, my crude experiment in recording who does what was a revolutionary approach to understanding home economics—more than a century and a half ago. The idea of quantifying household production dates to 1855, when a French sociologist, engineer, and economist, Pierre Guillaume Frédéric Le Play, published 36 monographs measuring men's, women's, and children's contributions to the family's livelihood by the number of days per year they dedicated to different tasks. Le Play didn't distinguish between paid and unpaid labor because most of his subjects existed outside of the industrial system, as farmers and small tradespeople such as blacksmiths, cobblers, or carpenters, occupations to which their spouses and children could make meaningful contributions. But by the time the idea was revisited in the twentieth century, both by Canadian economist Margaret G. Reid in her 1934 *Economics of Household Production* and later by Nobel-prize-winner Gary S. Becker in the mid-1960s, most men worked away from the home in factory, trade, or professional jobs, while many women were unpaid housewives. The United Nations System of National Accounts, established in 1947, only reflects one of these two spheres of activity, the one that can be measured in cold, hard cash—that of a nation's "productive labor" in the workplace.

Those two spheres collided in the 1970s. By then, women had entered the labor market en masse—over the decade, female wage earners in the USA increased by 50 percent, according to U.S. Bureau of Labor Statistics (BLS) data. They still, however, maintained primary responsibility for home and family. "Every woman basically knew that I've got two jobs, one that's for pay and one that isn't for pay . . . And that's not working for me," explains Karen Nussbaum, executive director of Working America and the 1993–6 director of the U.S. Women's Bureau. The subject of unpaid work began to gain traction in the women's movement. "A popular rallying cry was Wages for Housework," continues Nussbaum. "It was a global issue, too. It came up at the international conferences and so on. But it didn't have much purchase. It just seemed so far-fetched." Then, in 1988, Marilyn Waring, a renegade New Zealand politician turned activist, published *If Women Counted*, a 386-page fulmination arguing that the invisibility of most women's labor in national accounting systems had devastating consequences for them—and for society in general.

"If you are not visible as a producer in a nation's economy, then you're going to be invisible in the distribution of benefits. And wherever I was, this was the world situation for women," says Waring in the National Film Board of Canada documentary about her life. "I look at it [unpaid labor] as the single largest sector of any nation's economy, and the one on which all market activity depends," she told me. In her book, she made the case for quantifying this work in the only currency that made sense. "[T]he one common denominator that all of us have, the one thing that we might be said to choose to exchange that is our own, is time," she says in the film.

The attention to the issue in the women's movement and Waring's blunt call to action set off ripples around the globe. In 1991, the U.S. Congressional Black Caucus held a workshop on unremunerated work. Afterwards, Democratic Representative Barbara-Rose Collins of Michigan, a single, working mother herself, introduced legislation (and again in 1993 and 1995) tasking the BLS with gathering data about women's unpaid labor and calculating its monetary value. In 1994, Nussbaum, working closely with the White House, organized the Working Women Count! project which, through 1,600 community partners and a national media campaign, surveyed more than 300,000 working women about the problems they faced on the job.

"One of the questions that we asked was, what's the most important thing that the president needs to know about being a working woman? And the number one issue was balancing work and family," Nussbaum says. To explore what could be done, Nussbaum began a series of meetings with the director of the U.S. Census Bureau, economist Martha Farnsworth Riche. "There were a number of policy issues that surfaced— childcare, paid time off, the workplace side of the solution. But the home side was what would be addressed by this notion of wages for housework, and the first step for that is how do you quantify the unpaid labor women do?", explains Nussbaum. "That's the basis of the time-use survey."

"Much of the work we do is not valued—not by economists, not by historians, not by popular culture, not by government leaders," lamented Hillary Clinton in her opening address to the 1995 UN Fourth World Conference on Women, in Beijing. Time-use surveys were an explicit part of the platform that came out of that conference, directing nations to "[d]evise suitable statistical means to recognize and make visible the full extent of the work of women and all their contributions to the national economy, including their contribution in the unremunerated and domestic sectors." They are, like my refrigerator Post-its, an evidence-based tool to expose gender disparity—and its far-reaching repercussions.

The American Time Use Survey (ATUS), which began operations in 2003 and issued its first report in 2004 under President George W. Bush, does just that—without editorializing. (In fact, the USA was a latecomer to the party; almost all the Global North countries—Australia, the UK, the Netherlands, Finland, Italy, Israel, Germany, Austria, France, and Canada—were already collecting regular or episodic national time-use data.) But its statistics speak volumes. The most recent ATUS, in 2021, shows that while both sexes care for their homes, children, and elders, women dedicate 3.2 hours each day, 71 minutes more than men, to these unpaid labors of love. (Despite the perception that twenty-first-century men are more egalitarian than men of previous generations, the domestic duty divide has closed by only 14 minutes since 2003, the first year of the survey.) In the world of outside work, the situation is reversed. Both sexes labor for pay, but men clock an average of 4.18 hours, 79 more minutes than women, on the job each day. Whether women are sitting out the paid economy by choice—many women opt to stay home with babies and toddlers and try to be home after school when they are school-age—or circumstance, because they are unable to find full-time or well-paying work, there are serious consequences. These start with lower income and reduced access to health insurance and end with smaller social security stipends and less retirement savings, contributing to the feminization of poverty, especially for women of color.

The persistent discrepancy in men and women's participation in care work is especially sobering when you consider that we are now, unquestionably, in the era when men and women are most equal, a transformation brought about by the agricultural, industrial, and sexual revolutions of the past 150 years. Which prompts the question: Did they relieve women's burden—or add to it? Although no other American time-use survey has been as extensive or as regular as the one run by the u.s. Bureau of Labor Statistics, we can compare its recent findings to several one-time assessments to see how much the situation has changed over the twentieth century. In 1974, sociologist Joann Vanek published in *Scientific American* an article entitled "Time Spent in Housework," which collated some twenty local studies funded through the 1925 Purnell Act on how women budgeted their time, mostly conducted during the 1920s and '30s, with a 1965–6 national time-use survey done at the University of Michigan's Survey Research Center.

Vanek's findings were completely counterintuitive. Between 1924 and the 1960s, the time spent in housework for a woman without an outside job actually increased, from 7.4 to 7.9 hours daily, despite an influx of labor-saving appliances and devices such as refrigerators, dishwashers, washing machines, dryers, toasters, blenders, and vacuum cleaners and the tidal wave of prepared, convenience, and snack foods that was transforming supermarkets into the 40,000-item cornucopias they are today. (She speculates that higher standards of cleanliness, such as changing clothes every day, instead of once a week, negated any time savings.) It should be noted, however, that working women of the 1960s were less punctilious about their housekeeping, spending an average of only 3.7 hours. Throughout the period, although the time spent in food preparation and cleanup declined steadily, it continued—and continues—to be women's most time-consuming chore. In 1926, nonwage-earning women spent 3.2 hours in the kitchen every day; that dropped to 2.7 hours in 1968, and 1.7 hours in 2018.

Food preparation's association with inequality did not go unnoticed by twentieth-century feminists. Each and every one of the 28 times Betty Friedan itemizes the things that "confine," "burden," and add "drudgery" to women's lives in *The Feminine Mystique*, published in 1963, cooking topped the list. A decade later, food preparation still occupied four of the seven most unpleasant tasks in Pat Mainardi's 1971 essay, "The Politics of Housework." "Here's my list of dirty chores: buying groceries, carting them home and putting them away; cooking meals and washing dishes and pots; doing the laundry; digging out the place when things get out of control; washing floors."

Comparing data from around the globe and during the first fifteen years of the twenty-first century gives an even more depressing portrait of the state of gender equality. In 2019, economist and statistician Jacques Charmes, a frequent collaborator with the United Nations and the Organization for Economic Cooperation and Development, published a worldwide analysis of men's and women's paid and unpaid work. It shows a decidedly middle-of-the-pack position for the USA. *Unpaid Care Work and the Labour Market* ranks American men, with 168 minutes in 2017, seventh in the amount of time they dedicate to "unpaid care work," the UN's preferred term. However, American women, with 264 minutes, labor longer than almost half (30 of 72) of their counterparts in Europe, Asia, Africa, the Middle East, and the Americas.

American women can find scant comfort in the fact that we are not alone in shouldering a disproportionate responsibility for the smooth functioning of family life. Our unequal burden in cooking, cleaning, and tending others is part of an international pattern. "At the world level, women dedicate 3.2 times more time than men to unpaid care work: 4 hours and 32 minutes (272 minutes) per day against 1 hour and 24 minutes for men (84 minutes)," Charmes writes. For an average of 25 representative countries from 1998 to 2012, women's unpaid care work dropped by only 10 minutes; men's increased by a mere 13. Women's "free labor" has a high cost for our professional, social, economic, and political development.

* * * * *

For years, my sister-in-law María lived in the fourth-floor apartment she'd shared with Rafael and me in Quito during the 1990s. The remaining floors were occupied by three generations of a single family: grandmother under us, then middle-aged parents, and finally their daughter, her husband, and young son (who insisted on being called James Bond). Returning to it was like visiting an old friend. María had left our cheerful coffee mugs on the shelves over the long, stone counter in the narrow kitchen, and my red plastic market basket was still stowed underneath it. After breakfast and before the day's activities—visits with friends and relatives, sightseeing with our three children—I would go for an hour-long walk, revisiting the hectic commercial boulevards and quiet residential neighborhoods I'd crisscrossed as the owner of a small English-language newsmagazine. By late morning, the piercing Andean sun floodlit every detail: stucco colonial houses topped with terracotta roofs, modern poured-concrete houses with whimsically shaped doors and windows, and endless small gardens teeming with lantana, trumpet vine, and roses.

At that time of day, my roaming was also olfactory. The aroma of whatever was being prepared for *almuerzo*, hearty lunch, wafted outside most houses. I smelled simmering stews and soups, the slightly nutty perfume of rice, the mouth-watering scent of frying—potatoes, sweet and green plantains, and fish. If I tried, I could even detect the clean, vegetable odor of chopped tomatoes, cabbage, lime, and cilantro. The food smells made the neighborhoods feel welcoming, homey, and I contrasted it unfavorably with strolls in the United States, where the only time I ever smell cooking is Thanksgiving, and even then, only a handful of houses. As I had when I lived in Ecuador, I tsk-tsked in my head. Like many foodies, I believed that the decline in cooking was tied to our decline in physical health and social wellbeing, and that if this could be rekindled, it would improve our lives.

It took a month at the elbow of the cook on a South American hacienda, a large estate farm, to disabuse me of this nonsense. About fifteen years ago, I decided to give up a lucrative business doing public health research, development, and communications to make my fortune as a writer. My first project was to ship my entire family to Ecuador for a month so that I could learn the secrets of Andean home cooking with the best chef I knew, Carmen, who had worked for a relative of Rafael's since she was a young woman. I spent hundreds of hours with her in the kitchen, learning the hacienda's recipes and techniques (some from Rafi's aunt and some from Carmen's family), along with an ample dose of homespun wisdom, but in the end, the greatest lesson she imparted was in my own obliviousness to other people's pain and struggles. Only at the end of my stay did I learn that Carmen had incurable breast cancer and was valiantly trying to ensure that her daughter, Patricia, would have a better life—a life in which she didn't sleep in a small house "gifted" to her by her boss (instead of paying her a living wage) and which went far beyond raiding her own family's culinary heritage to keep a roof over her head and food on the table.

After my Slow Food denouement, my pre-*almuerzo* strolls in Ecuador were never quite the same. I was too aware of being from the Global North, of my privilege and infinite choices. Wherever I was, outside the luxury abodes of the elite, passing middle-class homes in Quito or Guayaquil, or going by ancient stucco houses of rural villages with their worn, bright paint, the crescendo of cooking smells limned the presence of hidden women—paid cooks, wives and mothers, grandmothers, aunts and daughters, and their lengthy preparations for the midday meal. Now I wondered, did they want to be there? What hopes had they hobbled? What dreams had they dashed?

Of all the work that goes into homemaking, there is no other time suck as greedy as cooking. On average, American women devote 52 minutes a day to food preparation and cleanup, according to 2021 American Time Use Survey (ATUS) data; men, less than half that. Being a mother increases meal ministrations, by just a minute for those with full-time jobs, to 68 minutes for mothers who work part time, and 102 minutes for mothers who don't have paid employment, according to combined ATUS data for 2013–17. Given the fact that most American kitchens sport refrigerators, stoves, toaster ovens, dishwashers, microwaves, and blenders, that U.S. supermarkets are crammed to the gills with prepared foods and convenience products, and that women's equality is at the upper end of the spectrum, I expected to find that the amount of time women spent on food preparation in the rest of the world would be substantially more than this hour or hour and a half. However, Charmes's UN time-use studies did not break down unpaid labor by task.

Not to be deterred from detailing just how much of women's lives are spent slicing, sautéing, and washing dishes around the world, in 2018, Robin Kanarek, then the John Wade Professor of Psychology in the School of Arts and Sciences at Tufts University, a small group of her students, and I decided to return to the original data for each country in a similar 2015 study, "Time Use Across the World:

Findings of a World Compilation of Time Use Surveys," to see if we could put together a global portrait of how much time women dedicate to dinner. (Does it bear mentioning that none of Professor Kanarek's male students signed up for the project?) To do so, we plunged into the wild and woolly world of comparative data. One country counted only women eighteen and over, while another fifteen and over, and another ten years and over. How to reconcile? Many of the Latin American nations tabulated their results by weekly, instead of daily, hours. Could we simply divide by seven or was it more complicated? Some countries followed the detailed breakdown of international time-use categories exactly; others included or excluded some of these in what they considered food preparation. And finally, for the many places that only had their files in native languages, we got creative with Google translator, first figuring out the correct terms in the other language, then searching the documents and then translating the passages or tables that turned up. After some false starts and some errors, we were able to extract cooking and dish-doing data for 52 of the original 65 countries in the UN study.

I supposed that as we worked, the students were absorbing the information about Ghana, Moldova, and Paraguay, and that was making them reflect on how the hours the women there put into nourishment affected their lives. So, at the end of the semester, I asked them how tasks were allocated in their own families. Who cooked? Who worked? Were their mothers happy with the arrangement? Although they came from different regions and backgrounds—American Midwest and West Coast; Jewish, Northern European, and

COUNTRIES AROUND THE WORLD WHERE WOMEN SPEND THE LEAST AMOUNT OF TIME ON FOOD-RELATED ACTIVITIES

Country	W Food Time	M Food Time	W/M Food Time Ratio	W—Unpaid Work Time/ Rank	W—Food Time/ W—Unpaid Work Time	GDP per Capita/Rank
USA	49.2	20.4	2.4	246/17	.02	$47,132/9
UK	54.0	27.0	2.0	232/12	.23	$36,298/21
Sweden	57.0	35.4	1.6	240/15	.24	$47,667/7
Denmark	58.2	33.0	1.8	243/16	.24	$55,133/5
Thailand	60.3	7.0	8.6	174/1	.35	$4,621/88
Finland	61.8	27.0	2.3	211/3	.29	$43,134/14
New Zealand	62.3	27.6	2.3	247/18	.25	$31,589/25
Norway	64.2	36.0	1.8	230/11	.28	$84,543/2
Canada	65.0	27.0	2.4	257/21	.25	$45,888/11
Austria	67.8	21.0	3.2	269/26	.25	$43,723/13

(in average minutes daily for total population)

Nigerian—I was struck by how similar their answers were. Each reported that their female parent assumed responsibility for all or most of the cooking; that they also had careers, working part time or taking time off while their families were young; and that they thought their mothers were just fine with it. Even though the arrangement is the same in my house, I was dumbfounded and dismayed.

But whatever the students thought, the numbers don't lie. Cooking's unpopularity can be attested to by attrition, both historical, as seen in the trends in the United States over the twentieth century, discussed above, and international. What we found was that the greater a woman's economic choices, the less time she spends cooking and doing dishes. In the USA,

COUNTRIES AROUND THE WORLD WHERE WOMEN SPEND THE MOST AMOUNT OF TIME ON FOOD-RELATED ACTIVITIES						
Country	W Food Time	M Food Time	W/M Food Time Ratio	W—Unpaid Work Time/ Rank	W—Food Time/ W—Unpaid Work Time	GDP per Capita/ Rank (of 180 countries)
Algeria	168.0	6.0	28.0	312/44	.54	$4,478/91
India	156.0	4.8	32.5	297/36	.53	$1,176/135
Tunisia	155.0	7.0	22.1	326/46	.48	$4,160/96
Pakistan	154.2	1.8	85.7	287/34	.54	$1,049/141
Mauritius	154.0	13.0	11.8	277/30	.56	$7,303/69
Albania	149.4	6.0	24.9	314/45	.48	$3,616/100
Turkey	145.8	7.2	20.3	371/50	.39	$10,207/57
Tanzania	144.8	16.6	8.7	212/4	.68	$5,43/162
Serbia	138.0	19.2	7.2	301/39	.46	$5,354/81
Romania	136.2	22.2	6.1	264/24	.52	$7,391/67

(in average minutes daily for total population)

the UK, Sweden, Denmark, Thailand, Finland, New Zealand, Canada, and Austria, the women give a low of 49.2 minutes to a high of 67.8 minutes daily to this activity. It also shrinks in relative importance in their total unpaid work, accounting for just 25 percent of daily minutes. These countries have some of the world's highest per capita incomes—and probably not coincidentally, the highest rates of happiness, according to the *World Happiness Report*—so we can assume that their actions are intentional. (One interesting exception, Thailand, will be discussed in detail later.)

Conversely, housewives in places such as Baddi Jhook, Pakistan, and Novi Pazar, Serbia, spend hours simmering *aloo josht*, a spicy meat and potato stew, or baking *podvarak*, sauerkraut casserole with meat and bacon. It's no coincidence that the nations where women are still slaving over the hot stove for a high of 168 minutes daily to a low of 136.2—Algeria, India, Tunisia, Pakistan, Mauritius, Albania, Turkey, Tanzania, Serbia, and Romania—are mostly low-income countries, as well as among the worst ranked for women's rights. (The only one where per capita income just squeaks into five figures is Turkey, at $10,207/£8,380.) Pakistan, where men spend a laughable 1.8 minutes a day on food-related activities, while women spend more than 2.5 hours, is ranked 151st of 153 countries for its gender gap in the 2020 World Economic Forum index.

Many of these women from Southern Europe, Northern and Southeastern Africa, and South Asia may love to make meals for their families, but it's hard to consider this the same choice—shaped as it is by economic hardship, traditional gender roles, reduced access to education, and, in some cases, the law—as can be made in the Global North, especially by the well-educated and affluent. "[P]reparing and serving food remains primarily women's responsibility which, if unfulfilled, can cause conflicts," explains Punita Chowbey, a researcher at Sheffield Hallam University, in an article. "For example, Ali found in Pakistan that if a woman failed to look after their house and prepare food, it led to domestic disputes . . . Charsley, in her work with migrant Pakistani husbands, shows that a wife who does not adjust her cooking to her migrant husband's preferences may be subjected to anger and violence within the marriage."

An uneducated housewife living in a rural part of the Global South can enjoy cooking. She may revel in selecting the best produce, meat, and staples; in the meticulous preparation and mouth-watering aromas; and in seeing her children, husband, and other relatives devour every last bite. But no matter how good she feels, she has little or no influence over her assignment as the primary food preparer for the household. Her life was already defined for her by her family, her village, her religion, her country. Refusal to comply could be devastating. She may be scorned, shunned, or cast out of her family. She may be hurt by her husband, father, or brothers. She may have to draw on extraordinary reserves of will and courage to leave, fend for herself in a strange city, find employment and shelter, protect herself from predators. In this severely curtailed agency, such a woman is like an enslaved person. Is cooking truly a choice when the cost of saying no is so great?

Would these women, if they could, join the rest of us in dumping dinner for more meaningful pursuits or simply more leisure time? We don't have to imagine their responses. Some representatives from these cooking-intensive cultures have spoken, through a sampling of field interviews conducted for research in sociology, anthropology, and other disciplines. The consensus: When women can leave food preparation behind, they do so without a backward glance.

I know a woman who uses [house catering] daily. She is a doctor and so is her husband, the children eat at her mother's house every day, but her food comes in a tiffin-carrier at 2 p.m. so she comes back for lunch, which is ready, and whatever is left over she takes for dinner.
  —Indian housewife (Caplan)

At some stages I feel the situation of my sisters very pathetic and poignant where they work from dawn to dusk having no acknowledgment . . . At few moments, I assisted my sisters in washing the floor and helped them out when they were cooking. I was amazed that even my mother scolded me and taunted that these are womanly jobs and men should not be involved.

—Young Pakistani man (Hussain)

My granddaughter doesn't even like the kitchen. The girls of today, they are very lazy to cook. I think they just want to be out. They rather go have a meal at the restaurant.

—Daria, Cape Town, 72-year-old South African widow (Baderoon)

In Pakistan we both never cooked. Initially after moving we had this problem, because when I cooked I took hours. Then he said if I spent so much time cooking when I will study. So he also started to learn cooking with me and now he does all the cooking as well cleaning up.

—Pakistani woman now in Britain with her husband (Chowbey)

I have stopped sending my daughter to school after Grade 5 because middle school is away from our village. My boy still goes to school using [a] bicycle but a girl would need to use public transportation that would cost me money. Besides I would need to give her five to ten rupees daily for her lunch that I can't afford.

—Pakistani man (Jamal)

I don't know if my son is going to find a girl [wife] who will be willing to cook for him in the way that I did. All the girls [women] these days are working and want convenience foods.

—Indian housewife (Caplan)

There are a few who pine for elaborate, home-cooked meals. They tend to be older women whose own lives revolved around family food preparation (if it's good enough for me, it's good enough for you), the men who enjoyed such meals, and upper- or middle-class women in the Global North who have chosen this role, temporarily or permanently, for themselves. Consider Elizabeth and Sammy, a same-sex couple in Durham, North Carolina, from Emily Matchar's 2013 book *Homeward Bound: Why Women Are Embracing the New Domesticity*, and their decision to grow, preserve, and cook their own provisions. The women "are both highly educated (Brown, Sarah Lawrence) and had plenty of career opportunities. But what they really wanted to be was 'stay-at-home, homeschooling, cooking, crafting mamas.'" This story illustrates nothing so much as the incredible luxury of having choices. And although I'm as susceptible as the next gal to retro fantasies of domesticity, I'd argue that we do ourselves and the world a huge disservice when we turn our backs on the immense resources invested in our educations and careers. Regardless of how many elites elect to make their own version of chef Mark Reinfeld's Blue Corn Crusted Tempeh with Shiitake Mushroom Gravy, the fact remains that most women around the world are housewives because they have no other option. And when they can, they extricate themselves the first chance they get.

Given that being liberated from the kitchen seems to be a fairly universal goal among women, what were the strategies used in the countries that cook the least? Three are readily apparent. Most of the countries are from Europe and North America and are among the world's wealthiest. They all have well-developed industrial food systems, which offer all sorts of convenience foods, from ready-to-eat, heat-and-serve, or pre-cut and pre-measured ingredients, sometimes assembled into meal kits. Relatedly, they have many restaurants, and at all price points, where people can either dine or carry out.

The same set of countries are those in which women's rights are most advanced: Norway, Sweden, Finland, and Denmark occupy places 2, 4, 3, and 14 on the World Economic Forum's 2020 ranking of the most egalitarian countries. Thus it's predictable that their men participate far more frequently in food preparation and cleanup than their counterparts in countries in which traditional cooking prevails. The ratio of the time men and women spend on food ranges from a low of 1.6 for Sweden to a high of 3.2 for Austria. (By contrast, these ratios climb to 6.1 for Romania and to 85.7 for Pakistan.)

Some of the Scandinavian countries deliberately promote these behaviors. "Equally shared housework tends to be common in Norway, whose work–family policy aims to increase the father's involvement in household labor through a range of policies and incentives," notes Arnstein Aassve and colleagues in a cross-European comparison. But even in these more progressive nations, differences remain in how men approach making meals. For example, history of technology professor Timo Myllyntaus found that Finnish men were bigger users of appliances such as the microwave, and he speculates that they are the reason why the country has a relatively high consumption of frozen, ready-made meals. To encourage such chore sharing, rather than expect their partners to cook traditional meals from scratch, perhaps women should tolerate such shortcuts—and even take advantage of them themselves.

There was one country on the list that broke the mold: Thailand. Thai women spend only 60.3 minutes per day on food preparation—and the least amount of time on housework of any women in the world. What's their secret? There are several factors that contribute to their successful divorce from kitchen drudgery. As do most Asian women, Thai women have high rates of employment, which gives them higher status and their own resources; in 2019, 59.6 percent of them had a job, comprising 45.6 percent of the labor force, according to the World Bank. Thailand hosts more than 250,000 legal (and probably many more illegal) domestic workers, many of them from neighboring Myanmar. "In the decades since World War II, it was common for urban middle class and elite households in Malaysia, Thailand and Vietnam to have servants, including cooks," says Penny Van Esterik in *Food Culture in Southeast Asia.* But it is in the food realm that the Thai system could really be a model for women around the world. Bangkok and many other areas have throngs of street vendors that offer whole meals or individual hot foods that can be purchased and brought home, giving rise to the term "plastic-bag housewife." "A household survey in 1990 revealed that households spent nearly half their monthly food expenditure on prepared food taken home or eaten away from home. Since 1990, consumption of prepared food has been steadily increasing," Esterik says. Finally, and crucially, Thais do not have a strong tradition of the sit-down daily dinner, so household members may serve themselves and continue their activities, and women don't feel they've shortchanged their families. "[E]ating 'a home-cooked meal' in a domestic setting does not appear to have the same cultural importance as it does in South Asia, or traditional Europe and North America," notes Gisele Yasmeen in her doctoral thesis on Bangkok's foodscape and gender relations.

* * * * *

The results of historic and modern time-use studies make one thing abundantly clear: A couple million years after female *Homo erectus* first skipped the hunting expeditions to tend the fire and the food, and despite the powerful countervailing forces of the agricultural, industrial, and sexual revolutions, women are still making meals for their mates and offspring. But today, instead of contributing to our species' progress, that role is slowing it. Around the world, women spend from a low of 1.6 times (Sweden) to a high of 86 times (Pakistan) the minutes that men do preparing food and washing dishes. In the Global North—the USA, the UK, Canada, and Scandinavia—that statistic hovers around 2.3 times. Globally, women average 100 minutes prepping, cooking, and cleaning up, while men, just 19. The mismatch between them is the hour or so a woman or girl could use to study, to work for pay, or to participate in civic, political, or professional organizations. A global survey by nonprofit Plan International found that a full 76 percent of almost 10,000 girls and young women aged 15–25 years old in 19 countries aspire to be leaders. Ditching dinner may just be the route to allow these hopeful young people to achieve that.

Given this, you'd think that there'd be a full-throated celebration of the freedom industrial foods offer, especially by the fairer sex. And while during the COVID-19 pandemic, when most people were trapped at home and—both from fear of shortages and nostalgia for their childhoods—stocking up on canned soup and corn, pasta, Grape-Nuts cereal, pickles, and Spam, there briefly was. But most of the time, when women have vocally embraced or even advocated these time-saving shortcuts, they've been attacked, starting in the 1950s with Poppy Cannon's punchy *Can-Opener Cookbook* and through the present era with Rachael Ray and Sandra Lee, television celebrities whose ready grab of the bag, box, or jar has earned them much ridicule, at least from the media.

In fact, just like Sammy and Elizabeth, a segment of the female population has ensconced themselves in the "new domesticity," concocting elaborate nightly dinners, baking from scratch, and even putting up their own preserves, chronicling their prodigious output on blogs such as "100 Days of Real Food" (discussed in Chapter One) or books entitled *Homemade With Love: Simple Scratch Cooking from in Jennie's Kitchen*. They—and their mostly male gurus (Michael Pollan, Jamie Oliver, Mark Bittman, and others)—shrilly deride those who don't make their own meals as lazy, ignorant, and selfish. This is both profoundly sexist and classist. In the twenty-first century, how we choose to eat has become a moral prerogative and, like many moral prerogatives, cloaks the nasty business of class warfare and social control. Most of these modern apron-donning ladies can afford not to work; their from-scratch doctrine thus becomes a disguised denigration of the unlucky indigent, whose turpitude is expressed in their greedy consumption of cheap packaged items and fast-food treats.

This disdain is deeply misguided and, by misdirecting our attention and energy, actively harms those we seek to help. Women may have cracked the glass ceiling, but they haven't gone through it. Most of us linger here on the underside, occupying fewer than 5 percent of the Fortune 500 corner offices, 20 percent of full professorships in the natural sciences, and "only 6 percent of partners in venture capital firms," according to Harvard Business School professors Francesca Gino and Alison Wood Brooks. We still earn only 80 cents for every dollar (80p for every £1) that men do, finds the National Partnership for Women and Families. Sexism? Maybe. But there's something each and every one of us can do in our own homes: measure how much time we spend preparing food and cleaning up after meals. Is it a half hour, an hour, an hour and a half? What would happen if you took that time and applied it to pursuing your dream of volunteering at an immigrant legal aid society, earning a master's in epidemiology online, organizing a political campaign, or writing this book?

4

SUBSISTENCE AGRICULTURE CHIC

"Hey, hey, Anastacia! Girls!" Zoe greets us, her infectious smile radiating across her dirt-smudged face. Gabriela and Mariela barely acknowledge her before they sprint off across the wide lawn bordering two large, rectangular fields. In their sights: their friends, whose mother works here every week, at the far side of the property. They are dragging large fallen branches from the adjacent woods to build a hut, a project which, judging from the hands-on-hips standoffs, entails a lot of conflict resolution. "How's Joshua?" I ask. "Good, good. He's really liking his new school." Zoe dismisses me with a gentle nod and edges toward the open barn, where people are selecting lettuce, peppers, carrots, eggplant, potatoes, and other vegetables piled in bins. The farm manager for our urban Community Supported Agriculture (CSA), she is painfully aware of every minute in her day and the unending list of tasks she must complete.

Zoe, who is in her early thirties, graduated from Yale College with a degree in history. While there, she worked in a New Haven hospital on a research project measuring the impacts of economic insecurity on children's health. Those whose families were most economically stressed tended to have children whose weight fluctuated according to their capacity to feed them. The experience inspired her—but not to work as a doctor, health researcher, or even policymaker. Zoe became fired up about growing local and organic vegetables and—somehow—getting them to the poor. While she was too early to have been influenced by Michael Pollan, she subscribed wholeheartedly to the vision of writer and sixth-generation farmer Wendell Berry, who preached sustainable agriculture, localism, and Slow Food—and who loathed processed food.

> The food industrialists have by now persuaded millions of consumers to prefer food that is already prepared. They will grow, deliver and cook your food for you and (just like your mother) beg you to eat it . . . The industrial eater is, in fact, one who does not know that eating is an agricultural act, who no longer knows or imagines the connections between eating and the land, and who is therefore necessarily passive and uncritical—in short, a victim.

Responding to this vision of ignorant consumers duped by the food industry who, if only they knew better, would make different choices, Zoe became a quiet evangelist for addressing inequality—environmental, health, social, and economic—by growing wholesome food and distributing (some of it) to low-income families and others in need. For more than a decade, she awoke before dawn and tumbled into bed shortly after dusk, working long grueling days at the farm. She planned crops, raised seedlings, fixed equipment (nursing along two elderly 1947 Super A tractors), paid bills, managed deliveries, wrote a beautiful weekly newsletter, and, yes, chatted with members. She subsisted on a $30,000 (£25,200) yearly salary—granted, supplemented by her husband's full-time, but not well-paying, job as a teacher—in one of the most expensive metro areas in the country. Along the way, she produced a green oasis, a convivial community, and close to 1 million pounds (453 T) of produce, both for CSA members and area food banks. Zoe is blazingly smart, fearsomely hardworking, and a role model for many around her.

Yet we must ask, is small-scale, diversified agriculture really the best use of her considerable talents? Is "fixing a broken food system" by laboring in the trenches as a farmer, butcher, baker, food truck owner, or chef the best use of an expensive education from one of the country's most elite colleges? (Or might it have been better utilized by one of the well over 30,000 well-qualified applicants Yale rejected the year she was admitted?) If her original goal was to ensure regular calories and better nutrition among the children of low-income city dwellers, was sustainable agriculture, which perhaps reached dozens or even hundreds of these truly heart-wrenching cases a year, the best way to do this? And, finally, does a disorganized patchwork of such endeavors make a meaningful dent in reducing the use of noxious pesticides, fungicides, and herbicides; in the western USA, the draining of aquifers and rivers; run-off polluted by chemicals and animal waste; agriculture's considerable carbon footprint (an estimated 11 percent of the world's total in 2013, according to the nonprofit Center for Climate and Energy Solutions); carbon sequestration; and even preservation of open space?

Probably not.

Returning to New York City always awakens a primal appetite in me. I travel there a few times a year to give talks, often by a low-budget mode I call the bus-by, in which I leave Boston mid-morning, arrive at the Port Authority or 9th Avenue gravel lot from which Go Bus operates, freshen my make-up in a public bathroom, and subway to my destination. After my presentation, I do the same thing in reverse, arriving home in the wee hours. During the day I purchase one large bottle of water and several cups of coffee. I eat almonds, apples, and chocolate out of my purse. Total cost for the trip is usually $40–50 (£33–42). But sometimes I splurge a little, and when I do, it's for the foods my paternal grandfather, born and raised here, and with a Sephardic taste for spice and heat, introduced me to as a child.

Which is how, one cold February trip, after I'd located the Museum of Food and Drink in Williamsburg, Brooklyn (half of my invitations emanate from this neighborhood, Ground Zero for the food revolution), I found myself wandering around looking for the coffee shop that a museum employee had assured me had a brew worth drinking, Florentina's Café on Graham Ave. On my way, I couldn't help but notice a large neon sign reading "Eat Real Food" in red, block letters outside what was obviously a converted garage. Once I'd recaffeinated, I'd investigate.

A gust of wintery air propelled me inside, still holding the paper cup of passable (OK, I'm a coffee snob) brew. I surveyed. The warm-up act was in the front of the store, a checkout desk with a small line and some desultory shelves stocked haphazardly with high-end kitchenware and staples.

In the back was the real show: a wide butcher case, behind which gleamed red, pink, and blue cuts of meat and trays of plump sausages in a variety of shapes and sizes. A small queue of customers had formed; they each held wire baskets with a few judiciously selected produce and baked goods—I imagined they shopped daily, like the French (used to) do.

Once at the head of the line, they had long, grave consultations with a jocular, white-apron-wrapped young man—the butcher, I assumed. Before I knew it, I'd ordered a juicy bratwurst. My consultation involved advice about where I could hunker down to eat it. In response, the counterman waved me up some stairs, where I slid onto a tall stool at a cooking island surrounded by pots and pans and dug in. As I munched the sausage—it was truly excellent—I learned a little more about my surroundings. I was in the shared space of the Brooklyn Kitchens, which offered cooking classes and related activities, and The Meat Hook, a bespoke butcher shop specializing in grass-fed animals from local farms. As staff darted in and out of offices, I relaxed and let the food and coffee create a sense of quiet wellbeing. Then I dusted the crumbs from my skirt and commandeered the 1970s-style bathroom (replete with homespun curtains) to brush my teeth, apply deodorant, comb my hair, and touch up my makeup. I squared my shoulders and marched off into the dark to give my talk.

As I walked, I observed the neighborhood, which, although it was obviously gentrifying in spots, still seemed true to its working-class roots. Directly across the Brooklyn-Queens Expressway from the artisanal meat shop was the Restaurant Comida Típica Ecuatoriana—spilling music, laughter, and the familiar smells of *primeritos* (soup course) and *segunditos* (main course), as well as the requisite *fritada*, crispy fried pork chunks, with *llapingachos*, potato pancakes stuffed with cheese. It brimmed with men, who I knew didn't earn much but were grateful for the chance to be here. To the south and east lay the neighborhoods of Bed-Stuy, a center for Black culture since the 1930s, and Bushwick, now major-ity Hispanic. Both neighborhoods have many families who live in poverty. Thinking of these people made me realize that there was something about my experience at The Meat Hook that was giving me spiritual indigestion. It wasn't the juxtaposition of the food-obsessed, educated, mostly white Brooklynites with struggling brown and Black neighbors. As someone who's lived in the Global South, I'm as tough-minded as the next person when it comes to watching people enjoy obscene wealth alongside destitution and suffering. No, what made me feel ashamed was that this gourmandizing was dressed up as virtue and perhaps led the fortunate to believe they had already done their bit to make the world a better place.

Awareness of and interest in food blossomed in the late 1990s and first decades of the twenty-first century. Once the province of Slow Food adherents and unsufferable gourmets, the message to eat local has percolated through American life. National and international grocery stores prominently label these fruits and vegetables and small-batch products in the aisles: "I'm a local." Many more people are not only choosing to eat this kind of food, as well as more plant-based cuisine, but choosing to grow or produce it. The vision of food activists is to create an alternate food system based on small-scale farmers and producers to replace, or at least complement, the industrial one.

While careers in the farm-to-fork movement may be spiritually fulfilling, they are materially unrewarding, to say the least, and as a whole create a less well-educated population that is both less likely to generate wealth and more likely to rely on state assistance. Agricultural and food-service workers are notoriously poor earners. Full-on farmers, ranchers, and other agricultural managers, jobs requiring a high school diploma or equivalent, had a median income of $73,060 (£61,340) in 2021, according to the U.S. Bureau of Labor Statistics. The macho chef (female chefs included; the restaurant kitchen is harrowing!), glorified in movies and television shows such as, well, *Chef*, *Master Chef*, and anything with the late, great Anthony Bourdain's imprimatur, pockets $50,160 (£42,100) per year. Butchers, the job *du jour* of every luxuriantly whiskered Brooklyn foodie, take home just $36,050 (£30,270). On the upside, there is "no formal educational credential" required, so if you hanker to break down beef loin into *noisettes*, you can avoid digging your financial hole any deeper by skipping higher education altogether.

Perhaps in part driven by their food-first outlook, young people have entered these occupations in droves. Millennials and zoomers, aged 20 to 34, made up 31 percent of all U.S. employment in 2021; more than three million of them hold jobs that have something to do with eating and drinking. About 900,000 are wait staff, with whopping annual earnings of $29,010 (£24,360). Some 600,000 are cooks, making about $29,120 (£24,450) a year. A total of 235,000 are food service managers at $59,440 (£49,900) and 298,000 are food preparation workers at $28,780 (£24,160) per annum.

Owning your own farm, bakery, small factory, or restaurant isn't much better. While the amount of money spent on food in the United States almost doubled between 1997 and 2014, to $1.459 trillion (£1.23 trillion), according to the USDA's Economic Research Service, food businesses are notoriously difficult. "A quick scan of the current state of the restaurant industry can make the restaurant landscape look a bit bleak: massive turnover, exorbitant labor costs, sky-high rent, punishing online reviews . . . the list goes on," confides dining software company Toast on its website. Business publisher *Forbes* explains how difficult it is to take an artisanal food business to the next level, both because of the challenge of securing large quantities of fresh ingredients in a market dominated by giant food companies and the knowledge, equipment, and operational changes needed for mass production.

Yet, despite these dismal economic prospects, American universities are increasingly peddling work in and study of the alternate food industry to their students. There are now more than thirty different food system and food policy degree programs at universities around the USA and (presumably) thousands enrolled in them. While a few of these graduates may find employment in academia, nonprofits, and government nutrition programs, it seems almost irresponsible to steer so many bright young people into low-paying, dead-end jobs, most of which score poorly on the economic multiplier scale.

Food-related businesses aren't engines of growth. In the 2014 U.S. Economic Census, only the Bay Area, New York

City, Boston, Seattle, and Portland had 3,500–9,000 food manufacturers, food stores, and restaurants. After these leaders, the total number of such establishments dips to between 2,000 and 2,500 for Denver and Providence, Rhode Island, then falls off a cliff. In other words, sustainable and artisanal food business thrive only in the economic wake of metropolitan areas booming with technology and professional service sectors, where jobs are high-paying, and consumers are rolling in cash and stock options. Subsistence farms and food-related micro-enterprises don't create prosperity; they feed off it.

Worse, channeling the newest generation into improving a "broken food system" wastes one of society's most valuable resources: youthful altruism, which, coupled with their willingness to take risks and ability to act without being encumbered by family responsibilities, can be a powerful force for change. The twenty-first century has presided over a large drop in volunteerism in the 18–34 age group, from 39 percent in 1997, to 28 percent in 2008, to 22 percent in 2015, according to data from the Statistical Abstracts of the United States and the u.s. Bureau of Labor Statistics. While there may be other causes, a belief that you can do good by growing organic produce; raising free-range livestock; hand-crafting pickles, sausage, cheese, wine, and other edibles; serving delectable locally and sustainably sourced restaurant meals; and, finally, simply eating them has surely contributed to the falling-off of the more traditional ways to improve the world. What about tutoring disadvantaged children? Working in shelters? Building trails? Visiting shut-ins? Or raising funds for aid abroad? Foodie-ism allows practitioners to justify their self-indulgence while turning away from the world's real problems.

Millennial author Eve Turow, who published *A Taste of Generation Yum: How the Millennial Generation's Love for Organic Fare, Celebrity Chefs and Microbrews Will Make or Break the Future of Food*, has an even more cynical interpretation of her peers' behavior. In an August 2015 interview in *The Atlantic*, Turow has this to say about the idea of a food-centric community as antidote to the long periods without face-to-face contact that many digital natives spend.

> [E]ven for myself, I had to look up at a certain point and say really, "Why am I posting this picture [of a kale salad]?" Is it for a sense of community or is it to show off? And if I was being honest with myself, it was a little bit of both, but mostly to show off. There's a commodity fetishism around organic kale at this point because we're using it as an identifier. We're using it as a signal of education, of knowledge, of income.

No comment.

* * * * *

In fall, when New England is ablaze and apple season is at its height, overripe fruit sometimes fall to the ground with a thud, where it is devoured by bees. The sound is soft, slightly muffled by the tall grass and loamy sod underneath. It is that same sound I imagine when I think about my maternal grandmother's father, who, when she was four, tumbled from an apple tree and broke his neck. He wasn't some weekend

pick-your-own-er, scrambling up the trunk for fun. Born
in the foothills of Vermont's Green Mountains, he was an
orchardist by trade, even traveling by train to Chicago with
his wares. (He returned with a carved wooden rocking
chair for my great grandmother, Emeline, which I have to
this day.) He lived for eight weeks, nursed by my mother's
"Manka," but his injury was too great. Minnie, who would
have been in her mid-thirties, was left a widow with eight
young children and a farm from which she managed to eke
out a living with a rotating cast of hired men. One of my own
Nana's earliest memories was of rows of cooling apple pies to
serve with cheddar cheese as part of the help's daily hearty
breakfast.

My grandmother got out first chance she got—as a
teenager. She boarded in town to attend the Brattleboro,
Vermont, public high school, returning home to visit her
mother on weekends and holidays. When she graduated, at
sixteen, she immediately got a job at the Peoples National
Bank as a teller. With her newfound riches, she outfitted herself with stylish clothes, cute hats, and dainty shoes; traveled
in the region; helped her mother; and socked away quite a
bit of savings. After a few years, she noticed a handsome new
face in a nearby boarding house: my grandfather, who had
recently graduated from the Albany College of Pharmacy
in upstate New York. Although he was, scandalously, five
years her junior, Nana didn't give a hoot. They married
and her stockpile financed the purchase of a drugstore and
a house. Then the Great Depression hit. My grandparents
postponed children—they were early and vocal enthusiasts
of the "rubber"—and my grandmother kept her post at the

bank, not leaving until she was 36 and pregnant with her first children, twins, who died after a day. The next year, at 37, she had my mother, and then devoted herself to parenting, bookkeeping for the pharmacy, and supplying the soda fountain with homemade sandwiches, cookies, and pies, for which she was justly famous. She helped her mother move to town, where she spent the rest of her days in a tall Victorian house with stained glassed windows and a beautiful yard full of flowers that is now a city park.

My favorite joke about my maternal grandparents' families, both from the same old New England stock, is that even though they've been here for more than three hundred years, they never amounted to much. In all that time, their greatest achievements were managing to hold onto their small plots and making enough to get by. There's nary a famous name among them—no wealthy benefactors, no accomplished professional men, no powerful politicians. Underlying the small success story of my grandparents' lives is their flight from the farm. My grandmother escaped her mother's destiny as a jill-of-all-trades and babymaking machine, thrust into panic mode by a violent accident. My grandfather ditched a chaotic household where his drunken father regularly beat his mother—who supported the family (and escaped her husband) by working as a cook in a nearby boarding school. After the ogre died, no doubt from cirrhosis, the family unearthed a whiskey bottle graveyard under the back porch. Despite her childhood trauma, Nana relished growing a tiny vegetable patch and luxuriant flower garden. Gagoo kept a safe distance from anything resembling soil, unless it was covered with turf grass and he was brandishing a 6-iron. They gave up their agrarian pasts without second glances.

Foodie-ism has recruited a new generation to return to the hardscrabble lives my ancestors finally escaped when my grandparents moved to town and joined the middle class—their daughter, my mother, even got a master's degree! Yet this is the very vision hawked by Michael Pollan in his various books from *The Omnivore's Dilemma* to *In Defense of Food* (to which the title of this tract refers) and others of that ilk. Unfortunately, it's nothing more than a false nostalgia for the preindustrial era, when small, diversified farms tended by strapping yeomen dotted the landscapes of the northern United States and Europe. But then we invented machines and built factories, which quickly filled with rural and immigrant laborers, hungry after crop failures at home or bone-tired from eking out a living from the land. As late as 1900, almost 41 percent of Americans still worked on farms; today that statistic is just 1.9 percent. In the same time period, agriculture, as a percentage of gross domestic product, dropped from 7.7 to 0.7 percent, according to the USDA's Economic Research Service. This transformation of the economy to one that was based on manufacturing and services was a very good thing. The cost of food went down. In 2018, Americans spent just 9.7 percent of their disposable personal incomes on food—5 percent on food away from home and just 4.7 percent for groceries. In 1960, they spent 16.8; and in 1901, an astonishing 42.5 percent. (Between 1960 and 1998, the average share of disposable personal income spent on total food by Americans, on average, fell from 16.8 to 10.1 percent.)

The result (at least in part)? Just like my maternal grand-parents, people saved money. Bought homes and cars. Went to college. Had enough leisure time to practice hobbies. In addition to my grandfather's beloved golf, Nana and Gagoo were avid bridge players and threw frequent parties at which people drank, danced, and created gossip fodder for the next day. My friend Zoe, and many other nouveau farmers, however, have found that the amount of time and energy required has turned them into reluctant adherents of Ben Franklin's rendering of the old English adage, "Early to bed and early to rise . . ."

Splintering the existing food system into countless small-scale producers will not only increase its complexity, but its cost to consumers—and possibly be a drag on the economy. Should we want further proof of the potentially damaging effect of a wholesale return to family-owned farms and artisanal food producers, there are many modern-day models to choose from. You might consult a millet farmer in Mali, where agriculture is 41.8 percent of the GDP, a corn tortilla *fábrica* owner in El Salvador (12 percent of GDP), or a rice paddy worker in Bangladesh (14.2 percent)—the very same regions that international nongovernmental organizations have been trying for decades to lift out of poverty. And what's the best way to accomplish this? A group of academic, government, and nonprofit experts convened in 2017 by the UN's Economic and Social Council found that "structural transformation, driven by growth in sustainable and inclusive industrialization, is the most effective driver of poverty reduction and economic growth in developing countries." The panel also emphasized the role of women's empowerment in lifting economies in China, Africa, and Latin America. On the flip side, they didn't shy away from pointing the finger at an international villain—agriculture:

> Poverty and hunger are concentrated in rural areas: 767 million people are extreme[ly] poor and 795 million are undernourished (SOFI, 2015); most of them living in fragile contexts and relying on agriculture for their livelihoods. Furthermore, about 8 out of 10 working poor live in rural areas and are engaged in vulnerable employment in the informal economy, mainly agriculture.

The formula isn't much different for Global North countries seeking to maintain their prosperity. The World Economic Forum identifies four broad factors—human capital, innovation, resilience, and agility—critical to a country's competitiveness. "The United States is the closest economy to the frontier, the ideal state, where a country would obtain the perfect score on every component of the index. With a competitiveness score of 85.6, it is 14 points away from the frontier mark of 100." The other countries in the top ten are Singapore (83.5), Germany (82.8), Switzerland (82.6), Japan (82.5), the Netherlands (82.4), Hong Kong (82.3), the United Kingdom (82.0), Sweden (81.7), and Denmark (80.6). This has resulted in economies with robust technology, services, and manufacturing sectors—even the United States, which has seen manufacturing contract since its heyday in the 1970s, still ranks third in the world in the environment and support it offers industry, according to a 2018 the Brookings Institution report.

Our food system is "broken?" Sure, we can improve the
healthfulness and quality of processed food and lessen its
impact on the environment, and we are. But only fools would
"fix" the cheapest, safest, and most abundant food supply
the world has ever known by replacing it with something
akin to subsistence agriculture. In fact, reuniting humankind
with the products of its labor is a Marxian fantasy—it's no
accident that the founder of Slow Food, Carlo Petrini, was
a communist political activist—rejected even by the world's
five remaining communist countries. Some of these still have
large and relatively unindustrialized agricultural sectors:
China's is 7.2 percent; Vietnam's, 14.7 percent; Lao's, 15.7 percent; and Cuba's, 3.8 percent, according to the World Bank, a
situation that they are eager to rectify. The USA's, by contrast,
is 0.9 percent. It borders on the absurd to think that redeploy-
ing our best-prepared young people into the food system is
anything but a blow to their and our growth potential.

* * * * *

"Here." Mami, Rafael's mother, handed me the ration booklet. "Why don't you go to the bodega with Carlitos?"(my
twelve-year-old nephew). I took Esmerelda's hand—she was
then a toddler—and followed his skinny legs as they hop-
hop-hopped down the front steps. We were several days into
a late 1990s visit to Cuba so that Rafi's parents could meet
their grandchild, a trip I made alone since he didn't think the
authorities would look kindly on the fact that several years
before he'd asked for and received United Nations refugee
status for political persecution and regularly published
anti-government essays. Carlitos, Rafi's oldest brother's son,

was excited to be with us alone and chattered nonstop about which video we would rent at the store after we'd picked up the family's daily allotment of bread. The bodega wasn't far, just a couple of sunny, palm-fringed blocks away and, when we entered, we were the only ones there. The walls were lined with long metal shelves, mostly empty. "Libreta," demanded the attendant, and Carlitos deposited the thin paper booklet in his hand. He marked off a couple boxes, handed it back, and scooped several beige rolls into our reused plastic bag. On the way back, we paused at the video store, where after a complex action versus princesses negotiation, we selected *The Aristocats*. At home, Carlitos gave the rolls to Mami. I asked if I could try one; it tasted as if it were made from ground-up stones.

Recently, I was invited to chat with a graduate food studies class at the City University of New York about how the u.s. military has influenced consumer food, the topic of my first book. I thought I would take the opportunity to better understand how people conceive of the food system and the role the food industry has in obesity and lifestyle diseases. The class was quite small and the students' fields diverse, ranging from sociology and quantitative methods in the social sciences, to women's and gender studies. The students shared the general public's deep suspicion of the food industry, which began with feeling they didn't understand the manufacturing process and ended with the view that they were being manipulated by its marketing. "All of the pro-cesses are very shrouded, and we're not really aware of what goes on . . . What pesticides are being used or not used, or [if they have] ethical labor practices, if they're being enforced.

Or what kind of preservatives and chemicals or vitamins are being added to my food—I'm kind of blind on that. That's all something that happens in the food system, but I don't know exactly what I've put into my body every day." While they acknowledged that overall, the system works: food is plentiful, inexpensive, safe, and available despite emergencies—as it was, for example, during the COVID-19 pandemic, they lamented that the food system "is not built to serve human interests but built to serve corporate interests." They talked scornfully about "the financial motivations of capitalist corporations . . . They want us to like it, they want us to eat it, they want us to need it, they want us to rely on it. So that it's integral, and we'll never stop buying it. And especially as, you know, urban dwellers, a lot of us don't have any other options. So, it kind of has us in a chokehold—you know, I can't grow things."

It was clear that they believe the American food system is riddled with malevolent actors and essentially designed to bamboozle consumers. Rather than reform, they advocate wholesale rejection. Which necessitates the question: with what would they replace it? The students weren't sure, but they knew that it would be a paradigm where food production was diverse, done on a small scale, and involved many (well-paid) people. "Growing food is like a communal activity that's important. That's not happening much anymore." When I asked them if they had any models—from the past or from other places—for a better kind of food system, most looked to the Global South. A vegetarian student said that she felt it would make people more accountable if people couldn't buy neatly packaged, pre-cut chicken breasts or ground hamburger in the supermarket. "I spent a lot of time in countries where a lot of people slaughter their own animals in their backyard. And that completely changes my opinion on eating meat. If you're gonna kill it yourself and participate in that way, eat your meat, but I think, you know, the current food system in America is just so removed from all things natural."

They also faulted capitalism for the patchy distribution of wholesome ingredients, resulting in food deserts where cheap, processed snack and junk foods are the norm. "I really would like to see wider distribution channels. I think food pantries, for example, should be government funded. And on every single corner, at least in the United States, regardless of the zip codes, wealth, or status." One student fantasized about "wav[ing] a wand and creat[ing] some magic [for] food insecurity issues, especially for people say, thirteen and under, because they're often at the mercy of their parents, whoever their caregiver is to, you know, be feeding them properly." Another student chimed in, maybe the United States could emulate "Cuba's system where they do have a minimum, everyone has like a minimum ration of food that they get, I don't know if it's every week or every month? There's complaints about it, and whatever. And it's not fixing the food system, but it's fixing food access, which is interesting. And something we could definitely do better on."

At the end of the session, I said, "So kind of shifting gears a little bit, I want to talk about obesity and lifestyle diseases. Why do you think Americans and many others around the world are overweight and obese and have an increasing rate of lifestyle diseases?" A mid-career student was circumspect, attributing it to a combination of factors, including inactivity and processed food. Another cited access—and sugar. "It's incredibly difficult to eat healthy if you don't have an abundance of resources. And also the fact that everyone's addicted to sugar, a lot of people drink drinks that have incredible amounts of sugar in them." Supersized portions also came up. I asked them how much responsibility the food industry had for our health problems. "Like, 97 percent," said one student, as most of the others nodded their heads. (Although later the older student dissented, estimating a more modest 50 percent.) I asked the first student to walk me through her reasoning.

"They just flood the market. They provide very little recourse for other alternatives. And food companies are not just food companies. They probably employ psychologists or people who are really able to understand how the brain works, how humans work, human nature, because they want you to want their product. So, there's focus groups, there's endless things to take a product to market. And the things that they're considering about the product is not their health value. It's its marketability, its desirability. The idea of how healthy foods are, or what this is going to do to the consumer, I feel like it's not even on the agenda . . . unless it's a product that is specifically being targeted to a health-conscious market, because that is a very large market with a lot of money to spend. The corporations that are looking at bringing products to the average American table are really not considering the health benefits of their products at all."

Well, no, they're not. And the reason for that is they are companies, and their primary purpose is to make money for owners or shareholders. That's not to say corporations can't consider other values—human health, environmental sustainability, rewarding workplaces, and fair trade—as they fight to stay ahead of the competition and expand market share. But they are not obligated to, and unless these public goods are enforced by government regulation, the results will always be piecemeal. The students had a rather mawkish vision of rural life and socialism in the Global South, but their concerns raise a valid point. If diet is important to wellbeing, shouldn't food companies be considering the impact of their products on their customers' health alongside turning a profit? While this might be difficult or impossible to legislate, there's another way to achieve the same end.

Enact policies that encourage food companies to become benefit corporations, a legal framework that requires them to consider social, environmental, and economic impacts in making business decisions. The designation is currently accepted in two-thirds of the American states and several countries, and a third-party certification process has been created through which participating companies can be evaluated, rated, and monitored. In the food industry, there are already dozens of benefit corporations, both certified and not, including Amy's Kitchen, Ben & Jerry's, Cabot Creamery, King Arthur Baking, Peter and Gerry's Organic Eggs, Tofurky, Plum Organics, and Danone North America. All it would take is a catchy consumer awareness campaign—"B Healthy" comes to mind—to accelerate the food benefit corporation trend among the public or, better yet, a couple of strategically placed federal regulations. For example, the Federal Communications Commission could limit food advertising to kids to that of certified B Corps; federal food purchasing programs, from the school lunch program to military rations, could require the classification as a prerequisite for potential vendors; and the Internal Revenue Service could offer tax incentives. Evil junk food companies could continue to push their addictive products, but at least they'd be defanged—clearly classified as unhealthy, limited in the places they could be used or sold, and paying more for their business model.

5

THE ELEPHANT IN THE ROOM

My tenth year was not a happy one. My family had just moved from a married student housing complex—my father went to graduate school at the ancient age of thirty—where the gated road teemed with playmates and games. The kids were a ragtag, international bunch, hailing from Mexico, Thailand, Israel, and Nigeria, as well as all over the United States. No one cared how old you were or whether you were a girl or a boy. The only important thing was to be able to run fast and for hours, as we spontaneously formed teams for tag, cops and robbers, hide-and-go-seek, kickball, whiffle ball, and street hockey.

But in the new neighborhood, there was no one my age, and while we had a house with a small fenced-in yard, the busy street was off-limits for sports. That year, my life narrowed to a dull but debilitating routine. After walking to and from the school about a half a mile away, I settled into an armchair, plowing through piles of library books and a family-sized bag of Nacho Doritos. By midyear, I'd accumulated an extra 25 pounds (11 kg). Even my new fashion statement—roomy engineer's overalls worn with a jaunty, red kerchief—couldn't hide the fact that

I'd propelled myself firmly across the line from stocky to chubby.

For decades afterward, I blamed my weight gain on the chips. With more than thirty ingredients, most of which were flavorings and dyes, almost half of total calories from fat, and diabolically engineered to override satiety, they seemed the most likely villain. Today, most experts and the public agree: Energy-dense junk foods are a modern-day scourge, supplanting traditional healthful foods with mindless and endless snacking that has layered us with lard. But true to my contrarian nature, I've begun to rethink my apocryphal Doritos-made-me-fat story. The truth, I suspected, had little to do with the actual foodstuff—I could have been pounding sticks of butter, the treat I helped myself to on baby's first trip to the grocery store—and more to do with the fact that I'd replaced hours of physical activity with hours of immobility and, relatedly, was consuming more calories than I burned. With this in mind, I began to revisit our sanctimonious horror at processed food in general and "junk food," with its minimal nutritional contribution, in particular.

"Since 1960, the prevalence of adult obesity in the United States has nearly tripled, from 13 percent in 1960–1962 to 36 percent during 2009–2010," states a Centers for Disease Control (CDC) study. From that point, the obesity rate has continued to climb, reaching 42.4 percent of the adult population in 2017–18. Could this well-documented worldwide widening of the waistline be my story writ large (groan)? Let's take a closer look at industrial food from a health perspective, to see if there's any evidence that it has special obesity and disease-imparting qualities, or if the problem is as simple as it's always thought to have been: eating too much and moving too little.

Opponents claim processed food is brimming with deleterious substances. These come in two general categories. First, some specific ingredients, such as sugar and high-fructose corn syrup (HFCS) or fat, saturated fat, and trans fat are said to have unique properties making them harmful over and above their caloric contribution. Second, practically any additive that has a polysyllabic name is viewed with suspicion and fear by the public, food activists, and many researchers—in fact, pretty much anyone who isn't a food scientist or technologist! Happily, most of these assertions have proved to be untrue.

Although there have been exhaustive studies, scientists have mostly been unable to document a special obesity-inducing quality, or, with one exception, an incontrovertible disease link, in specific foodstuffs. (The one exception is trans fat, the unnaturally shaped molecules of which stud arterial walls and contribute to plaque formation.) For years, fat, and especially saturated fat, was the villain *du jour*. A post-Second World War spike in heart disease was attributed to the good life enjoyed by the white-collar professionals who shuttled between their urban offices and suburban homes in zaftig automobiles; wooed clients with three-martini, steak, and *pomme frites* lunches; and on weekends participated in endless rounds of competitive cocktailing and grilling. The bottom began to fall out of that theory at the turn of the twenty-first century, when researchers, whose biochemical identification tools now allowed them to differentiate among a whole range of blood molecules, found that intake of saturated fats, while it might increase total cholesterol, didn't necessarily correspond to increases in the least healthy types of molecules (low-density lipoprotein, LDL). Health authorities, while they haven't advocated a wholehearted return to smearing pats of butter on everything, now suggest people include ample healthy fats, such as those from plants and fish, in their diets.

More recently, blame has turned to sugar. There are two accusations. First, that fructose, which is metabolized by the liver, also damages it, and increases blood cholesterol and insulin resistance. Fructose is used widely in soda and as a sweetener for bakery products and condiments. Says George Bray, one of the founders of the field of obesity studies,

> Nonalcoholic fatty liver disease did not exist when I was a medical student. It appeared in the 1980s, and it is now a significant precursor, if not the leading one, of end-stage liver disease and liver transplants. The consumption of soft drinks had doubled by the 1980s. This suggests to me that the rising intake of fructose in soft drinks could play a role in the development of nonalcoholic fatty liver disease.

The other allegation is that sugar, because it is so calorically dense and easy to consume—think the aforementioned soda and fruit juices—contributes disproportionately to obesity.

The United States, unlike the European Union and the international community, doesn't have a central scientific authority that can help resolve complicated debates. Instead, it lets the market decide, which often means that the bigger an organization's budget, the louder its voice. Nutritional science is especially hazy. Academic, government, nonprofit, and industry studies duke it out unrefereed in a Wild West atmosphere, made all the more confusing by the paid public-relations gunslingers who fire diversionary shots into the crowd. These are not just the obvious food industry interests; the public needs to be wary of information coming from the pharmaceutical industry, some of the medical establishment, obesity experts, and the writers whose livelihoods depend on selling us diet books and programs. (Ironically, the only industry whose stake in our wellbeing matches our own appears to be the health and life insurance businesses, which stand to lose money from our ailments and untimely demises.)

For all these reasons, when presenting the current state of the science on sugar, it makes sense to rely on the staid World Health Organization (WHO), which has a careful and transparent process for developing, vetting, and getting non-profit and industry feedback on its recommendations. The 2015 WHO sugar-intake guidelines do not address the fructose controversy, so we will ignore this until they do, but they do recommend that no more than 10 percent of total calories be from "free sugar." This category includes both added sugars and the natural sugars in fruit juice; it should also be noted that the clearest causal relationship the WHO found with sugar was with dental caries, not, as they are now called, noncommunicable diseases (NCDs) such as diabetes and heart disease. The case for an indirect relationship between sugar and NCDs is as follows: a diet high in added sugars makes it easier to gain weight, which can lead to obesity, and the obese are more likely to become diabetic. But even the link between added sugars and obesity isn't certain. When an Australian nutrition researcher at the University of Sydney, Jennie Brand-Miller, who helped create the glycemic index, analyzed national data, she found that between 1995 and 2010–11, intake of added sugars and sugar-sweetened beverages dropped by 10 percent in men, 20 percent in women, and even more in children, while obesity increased. This finding, so discordant with current public policy thinking, led to her being attacked—although ultimately forgiven—by other scholars.

We could have saved ourselves about half a century of research, but it appears that a calorie is a calorie, no matter what its source. A 2018 meta-analysis by researchers in Australia and China of twenty studies worldwide found that there is no difference between low-fat and high-fat diets in terms of weight gain in metabolically healthy overweight and obese people—and a mixed difference (part good, part bad) on blood lipids. Similarly, a 2017 Norwegian study found that nutrient proportion—high fat/low carb versus high carb/low fat—doesn't matter; you lose weight (and flubber) and prevent diabetes when you reduce caloric intake, period. There is no demon ingredient (or foodstuff, although best to limit sugary juices and sodas) responsible for our roly-poly selves—and, by extension, no evil food industry conspiracy to make us fat.

But if the devil isn't in the ingredients, perhaps it's in the additives? Again, widespread consumer alarm at laboratory-fabricated food add-ins is largely unwarranted. Food additives come in four functional categories: flavor, color, conditioning (to aid in processing or impart a specific characteristic), and preservatives. Other substances end up in small quantities in food because of agricultural processes, treatment to prolong the raw material's freshness and rid it of harmful microorganisms, and the mechanical and chemical techniques used to create edible products. The u.s. Food and Drug Administration (FDA), the agency that oversees what companies can put into food, has a list of more than 3,000 common additives. When they are known or suspected to have negative health impacts, they are allowed only in minute quantities, a few parts per million. In addition, there are about 1,000 or so additives that are Generally Recognized as Safe (GRAS) by the FDA and can be used without restriction.

The European Union has more stringent regulations than the United States, prohibiting a few more additives and requiring that labels state when products are made from genetically modified organisms (GMOS). But, on balance, these differences are small. "Most substances added to food [in the United States]—even ones with long chemical names—are safe," says the Center for Science in the Public Interest (CSPI) in a 2017 report on "clean" food labels. It goes on to note, however, that some are not, and others are poorly tested. But even with that caveat, there are only a handful of additives that are legal in the United States, but not in the European Union, noted below.

Azodicarbonamide (ADA): A softener and whitener for dough. Used mostly by quick-service restaurants such as sandwich and burger chains. During baking, it breaks down into chemicals that cause cancer in laboratory animals.

Butylated Hydroxyanisole (BHA) and Butylated Hydroxytoluene (BHT): Flavor enhancers and preservatives. Considered a likely carcinogen by the U.S. government.

Brominated Vegetable Oil (BVO): Used to bind ingredients in citrus-flavored sodas and sports drinks. May contribute to body burden and affect memory, skin, and nerves.

Potassium Bromate: A rising aid and whitener used in bread and other bakery products. A possible human carcinogen.

Red Food Dye No. 40 and Yellow Food Dyes No. 5 and No. 6: Used in Europe with a warning label that may affect activity and attention of children.

The primary concern about this tiny list is decidedly old-school—cancer, with cognitive issues a distant second. None has been fingered as a magical obesity, cardiovascular, or metabolic-disease catalyst that somehow transforms the body into a fat-hoarding machine. (If you want to worry about what's in your food, maybe mull over some of the toxic byproducts of cooking, including acrylamide, PAHs (polycyclic aromatic hydrocarbons), and nitrosamines, and the short chains of synthetic polymers that migrate in from packaging.)

* * * * *

For further proof that processed food, in and of itself, doesn't make you sick, let's return to the 2018 global analysis of food preparation habits in 52 countries I conducted with Dr Kanarek at Tufts. After the students extracted the cooking and dish-washing data from the reports of each country's statistical bureau, I correlated it with WHO disease prevalence for the same countries and the same or similar years. If industrial food is the root of all that ails you, and home food is a cure, we would expect to find that those places with the lowest rates of obesity and death from diabetes and heart disease would be where people cooked everything from scratch. Is that the case? Hardly.

If we choose the United States as an unhealthy baseline, with 64.8 percent of its adult population overweight or obese, a diabetes-related death rate of 13.6 per 100,000, a heart-disease-related death rate of 67.2 per 100,000, and a 24.8 percent smoking prevalence during the study time period, which countries had even higher rates? Only two of the ten countries where women cook the least: Finland, which has a markedly slimmer overweight/obesity rate of 55.9 percent but similar smoking rate of 23.5 percent, a diabetes death rate of 4.4, and a heart disease death rate of 88.1; and Austria, which although slimmer still with an obesity rate of 51.8 percent, has a markedly higher smoking prevalence of 35.7 percent. The Austrians have a diabetes death rate of 14.6 per 100,000, and a heart disease death rate of 70.3.

Conversely, although half of the countries in which women cook the most are missing health data, three of the five that do have far worse cardiovascular and metabolic health indicators than the United States. In Mauritius,

DIABETES AND HEART DISEASE IN THE COUNTRIES WHERE WOMEN SPEND THE LEAST AMOUNT OF TIME ON FOOD-RELATED ACTIVITIES

Country	Women's Food Preparation Time (Minutes Daily)	Over-weight/ Obesity Rate (%)	Diabetes Death Rate (per 100,000)	Heart Disease Death Rate (per 100,000)	Smoking Prevalence	Inactivity Prevalence
USA	49.2	64.8	13.6	67.2	24.8	32.4
UK	54.0	60.6	4.4	57.6	27.2	37.3
Sweden	57.0	53.9	8.0	58.1	23.1	28.7
Denmark	58.2	53.3	11.0	40.7	24.7	24.3
Thailand	60.3	26.7	10.4	19.8	21.7	14.8
Finland	61.8	55.9	4.4	88.1	23.5	23.5
New Zealand	62.3	62.7	10.8	66.1	20.0	39.8
Norway	64.2	55.7	6.5	45.9	26.9	25.8
Canada	65.0	61.2	10.6	50.8	18.4	23.2
Austria	67.8	51.8	14.6	70.3	35.7	23.8

despite being relatively slim at a 29.3 percent overweight/ obesity rate and a 22.6 percent smoking prevalence—similar to that of the United States—the diabetes death rate is a staggering 171.4 per 100,000, and the heart disease death rate is 88.5. In Turkey, where 63.1 percent of the adult population is overweight and obese and a considerable 30.8 percent smoke, death rates from diabetes and heart disease are 25.2 and 63.8, respectively. Serbia has similarly elevated statistics: 54.3 percent of adults are overweight or obese and 42.1 percent of those over 15 years old smoke cigarettes; death rates from diabetes and heart disease are 21.3 and 82.1, respectively. In

DIABETES AND HEART DISEASE IN THE COUNTRIES WHERE WOMEN SPEND THE MOST AMOUNT OF TIME ON FOOD-RELATED ACTIVITIES

Country	Women's Food Preparation Time (Minutes Daily)	Over-weight/ Obesity Rate (%)	Diabetes Death Rate (per 100,000)	Heart Disease Death Rate (per 100,000)	Smoking Prevalence	Inactivity Prevalence
Algeria	168.0	57.4	N/A	N/A	15.2	34.4
India	156.0	16.5	N/A	N/A	14.3	13.4
Tunisia	155.0	57.8	N/A	N/A	31.7	23.5
Pakistan	154.2	24.2	N/A	N/A	21.3	26.0
Mauritius	154.0	29.3	171.4	88.5	22.6	25.2
Albania	149.4	53.3	0.3	60.0	31.2	N/A
Turkey	145.8	63.1	25.2	63.8	30.8	32.8
Tanzania	144.8	23.8	N/A	N/A	17.1	6.9
Serbia	138.0	54.3	21.3	82.1	42.1	38.7
Romania	136.2	54.5	6.6	21.3	32.8	25.3

each of those countries, women dedicate between two and a quarter to two and a half hours a day to preparing food for their families.

Let's not be disingenuous. What's going on in these countries has little to do with whether they're ladling traditional dishes onto a plate or hitting the drive-through after work and everything to do with wealth. (And smoking!) In fact, a 2017 study by over two hundred medical researchers around the world and published in the *Journal of the American College of Cardiology* found that the strongest correlates with death rates from diabetes and heart disease are social and demographic: income per capita, educational attainment, and fertility rates. The scientists found that death rates from cardiovascular disease, especially from ischemic heart disease, were consistently higher in low- and middle-income countries. They start to decline when nations reach a certain level of economic development. This is the exact opposite of the affluenza hypothesis that abundance and indolence breed lifestyle diseases.

Should food activists wish to continue to argue that from-scratch cooking has a salutary effect on health, let's examine the five countries with the highest rates of diabetes and heart-disease-related deaths in the world. Are any of the countries where women spend the least amount of time in food preparation and cleanup, an advantage admittedly not only conferred by prepared and convenience food, but by the availability of moderately priced takeout (hello, Thailand) and more egalitarian arrangements when it comes to chores (hats off to the Scandinavians), among the least healthy? Not a one.

It doesn't seem that eating home-cooked meals makes much of a difference, at least when it comes to cardiovascular and metabolic diseases. In the five countries with the highest rates of diabetes-related deaths—Mauritius, Mexico, South Africa, Armenia, and Panama—women cook from a low of 82 minutes per day in Panama to a high of 154 in Mauritius. Similarly, in the five countries with the highest rates of heart-disease-related deaths—Moldova, Kyrgyzstan, Lithuania, Armenia, and Latvia—women hunker down over their ovens for a low of 88 minutes in Latvia to a high of 121 minutes in Moldova. No one is any better for it for the two simple reasons that people get fat when they eat more

LEAST HEALTHY COUNTRIES IN THE WORLD						
Country	Over-weight/ Obesity Rate (%)	Diabetes Death Rate (per 100,000)	Heart Disease Death Rate (per 100,000)	Women's Food Preparation Time (Minutes Daily)	Smoking Prevalence	Inactivity Prevalence
FIVE COUNTRIES WITH HIGHEST DIABETES-RELATED DEATH RATES						
Mauritius	29.3	171.4	-----	154.0	22.6	25.2
Mexico	61.7	91.6	-----	103.0	17.1	26.0
South Africa	49.9	64.7	-----	87.0	21.0	46.9
Armenia	51.3	37.2	-----	115.0	29.3	N/A
Panama	55.2	27.5	-----	82.0	8.5	N/A
FIVE COUNTRIES WITH HIGHEST HEART-DISEASE-RELATED DEATH RATES						
Moldova	49.2	-----	371.0	121.0	23.9	12.3
Kyrgyzstan	44.2	-----	332.0	102.0	26.6	13.3
Lithuania	57.6	-----	223.0	101.0	31.1	18.4
Armenia	51.3	-----	208.0	115.0	29.3	N/A
Latvia	55.8	-----	191.0	88.0	37.5	22.0

calories than they burn, no matter what the macronutrient content of the food and if it was prepared in a home kitchen or on a factory floor, and diet isn't the most important factor contributing to their health.

* * * * *

I don't know about you, but there are a lot of things that keep me up at night: paying the bills, random acts of violence and terrorism, finding my next consulting job, paying for college, school shootings, the rise of American nationalism, growing income disparity, homelessness, saving for retirement, being displaced from my consulting job by artificial intelligence, fire, climate change, the next pandemic, financial market meltdowns, missing writing deadlines, that my husband or I will accidentally mow down a bicyclist and lose our house and our meager savings in a lawsuit, losing our health insurance, failing. It's fair to say that the world is in one of its more precarious moments and in the face of that instability, most of us have a single impulse: hide.

And what more soothing place to retreat to than the details of a complicated diet? My brother omits fat from his, swapping in liquid egg whites and skinny cheeses and eating chicken, chicken, chicken. Our friends Mira and Geoff read *Wheat Belly* and are no longer consuming carbohydrates. (I refrain from pointing out that they are no longer eating simple carbohydrates; vegetables have plenty of complex ones.) They have lost weight, and they feel great! When they were eating wheat, their minds just felt so clouded. Their contribution to our potluck—a delicious roast cauliflower with Indian spices and uncooked, sugar-free butter-and-cocoa cookies. My brother-in-law, and now my sister, are adherents of intermittent fasting, which they believe amps up their insulin sensitivity, preventing diabetes. (I'm guessing having two super hangry owners has made the work environment in their small architecture business delightful.) My cousin NayNay—understandably careful after a bout of cancer—and friend Diana, both longtime committed vegans, have gone the extra mile and followed the *New York Times* one-month sugar detox. Now that they are no longer being poisoned by sweetness, whole foods taste so much better.

And their blood sugar levels are no longer constantly spiking, keeping them on a Zen-like keel throughout the day.

The friends and relatives I've had that have lost weight/ gained energy/improved their mood/cleared their skin by adhering to, variously, gluten-free, keto, vegan, high-protein, and other nutritional plans are too numerous to count. Substitute some religious terminology for the foodstuffs they abstain from and you've got yourself a conversion experience: After sinning by huffing bread and rice, mainlining fried and fatty foods, or gorging themselves on cake and candy, the individual is enlightened by one of the dozen or so food gurus—the almost all-white, all-male pantheon includes Michael Pollan (eat only whole foods), Robert Lustig (no sugar), Gary Taubes (no sugar), William Davis (no gluten), Jason Fung (intermittent fasting; at least he's Asian—and Canadian), and Robert Atkins (no carbs; high fat and protein), each of whom advocates their particular brand of wellness philosophy. After following strict rules, the person is saved. This sort of asceticism is nothing new: The spiritual glow one gets from self-denial is part and parcel of all major world religions, from Christianity and Judaism to Buddhism and Islam. But what is unique—at least in this day and age; the ancient Greeks practiced it as part of athletic training—is its cooption for secular purposes and downgrading of the quest for spiritual transcendence to mere physical wellbeing.

Several years ago, I abruptly lost hearing in the upper ranges in both ears. I saw an otolaryngologist; a radiologist; a neurologist; two neurotologists, specialists in the neurology of the inner ear; and got tested up the wazoo (short list: Lyme disease, diabetes, syphilis, HIV/AIDS, lupus, rheumatoid arthritis, sarcoidosis, allergies), but no one could figure out what was wrong with me. So, I did what we all do in times of great stress, I put my faith in a higher power—the Internet. If I googled long enough and with the exact right combination of search terms, I would magically discover my diagnosis, and, with luck, the cure. Which is why from Friday, October 28, 2011, 9:38 a.m. ET, the moment I read about "secondary endolymphatic hydrops," in which an increased volume of inner ear fluid presses on the cochlea and (balm to my drug-fearing soul), which can be controlled with a special diet, I decided to stop eating salt and sugar—ruling out any kind of processed food.

The special diet didn't restore my hearing but following it for a month opened my eyes to how pervasive industrial food really is. I'm a relatively healthy eater, although under duress I'll concede that only a third of my calories come from whole or from-scratch food and the other two-thirds from sweets and treats (chocolate, ice cream, crackers, chips, olives, cheese) or the stuff that in a distant time or place would be relegated to the family pig—pizza crusts; half-eaten sandwiches; sad little ketchup-dabbed chicken nuggets. By noon of my first day on the regime, I was already panicked. What would I eat? I swung open the refrigerator and gazed longingly inside. Vast swaths of edibles, all off limits: frozen pizza, pot stickers, deli meats, cheese, condiments, peanut butter, jam and jelly, pickles. I slid open the vegetable compartment—lettuce, carrots, celery. A start. But what about the substance? A sprinkling of unsalted sunflower seeds? My stomach growled. How about an egg, crisply fried in a pool of butter? Scratch that, the butter has salt. Oh dear.

I was going to be hungry. Very, very hungry. Over the course of that month, I didn't lose weight, have more energy, or feel happier. In fact, I felt grumpy, tired, and deprived.

The experts are still arguing about the causes of lifestyle diseases. The most circumspect scientists say their origins are multifactorial and include access to medicine and medical interventions, smoking, alcohol, diet, and physical activity. But this is a cop-out. It may cover your posterior when it comes to medical malpractice, but the world has an urgent need for more exact information so that it can improve quality of life and reduce premature death for millions. Can't we assign a weight to how much each of these factors contributes? (Smoking's devastating influence is, after decades of disinformation from the tobacco industry, finally irrefutable, so on that factor, at least, discussion closed.)

For example, it's clear that access to medical care is probably the single most important thing we can do to save lives. While the countries with the highest rates of diabetes and heart disease are all over the map when it comes to obesity, smoking, and physical activity, they are unified by one thing: their lack of infrastructure, including healthcare systems. Tragically, we don't even need to point to these low- and middle-income illustrations; we can just compare the United States to its two closest peers, Canada and the United Kingdom. Despite having similar economies and cultures, the United States has a higher death rate for both diabetes and heart disease. (It should be noted that Brits have higher rates of smoking and inactivity than Americans, while Canadians have less.) What's one of the biggest differences among the three English-speaking nations? The United States has no national health system, meaning that some Americans have no insurance and others are footing mind-bogglingly large bills for hospitalizations and medications. The result, especially when combined with disparate rates of non-communicable diseases for those with low incomes and communities of color, led to the shocking spectacle of one of the wealthiest countries in the world having the most deaths during the COVID-19 pandemic.

During the late twentieth and early twenty-first centuries, Hippocrates' famous (and apparently misquoted) dictum, "Let food be thy medicine, and medicine be thy food," has been tossed about like rice at a wedding. But no one has been able to prove it. Yet we spend countless hours and billions of dollars on weight loss schemes or special nutrition. If a "good diet" is not the powerful panacea people imagine—an inviting illusion, because who doesn't enjoy thinking about food and eating it?—then we are wasting vast amounts of resources and endangering lives. A December 2019 PubMed search for the terms diet, nutrition, and food, along with cardiovascular, diabetes, heart disease, and obesity, yielded 303,371 results. A search of three terms related to physical activity and the lifestyle diseases turns up about half that, 189,663; smoking, 102,951; and alcohol, 38,620. But a search for healthcare access and the same terms, just 5,501.

One of my favorite thought experiments is to imagine I'm viewing my family from afar, like a child peeping in through the roof of a dollhouse. Since Rafi and I work from home, that looks something like this: significant other sits for hours on end in an office chair, then eats, and reclines for several more hours on a couch. Then he goes to bed. This may be punctuated by driving the car to drop off or pick up a teenager, a trip to the supermarket or Home Depot, gardening or home repairs, or a photography shoot. (Not to cast stones; my day is about the same, but I do run faithfully for forty minutes to an hour.) My two youngest daughters' activity logs aren't much better. Both practice a seasonal, travel-team sport—soccer and gymnastics—with plenty of aerobic conditioning, but it's another story during the off months. They take the bus to school, maybe do an extracurricular activity, and take the bus home (or more often, plead for a ride). In the house, they sit at their desks, lie on their beds, sit at the counter, and lie on the sofa. For all of us, most of these activities take place within inches or feet of a screen-based electronic device. Tell me your day is any different.

During the early to mid-twentieth century, the automobile, factory mechanization, and domestic appliances reduced the amount of time people spent moving their bodies. But Americans truly settled into their stationary ways with the arrival of the television. By 1970, 95 percent of homes had a set and the average person sat transfixed by it for six hours daily, according to the Statistical Abstracts of the United States (SAUS). Still, because programming could only be watched at certain hours and channels were few, adults still did other recreational activities—bowling, knitting, and reading—and children still played outside, as we did in my neighborhood in the mid-1970s. (Although I remember some long, open-mouthed television-viewing sessions, mostly cartoons.) Unfortunately, this period was relatively idyllic compared to the present era.

Since the mid-1970s, our love affair with screens has grown at warp speed. Without diminishing our ardor for television, the consumption of which rose to more than seven hours daily in 1990 (SAUS), electronic entertainment options exploded. In 1975 the video game Pong, played through a console attached to the TV, was released. Its raging success spawned an industry that today shows no sign of abating. But prying controllers, and later joysticks, out of the hands of frenzied adolescents would be fruitless. Other electronic toys were popping up like prairie dogs. In the mid- to late 1970s, home video recorders (VCRs) began to allow people to watch feature-length movies in their own homes. In the same period, the very first personal computers, the clunky Commodore PET and the Apple II, began to be sold in tech centers across the nation—by 1984, 8.2 percent of homes had a computer, according to the U.S. Census. That same year, the Cable Act removed regulatory barriers from cable television, and channels proliferated; some experimented with deliberately provocative talk shows, a format that stuck; these broadcast shoutfests are now as mainstream as the nightly news once was. (Let's not forget MTV, whose three-minute music videos foreshadowed YouTube's commitment-averse format, which rarely lasts for more than ten minutes.) And we haven't yet arrived at the biggest transformations—and continual captors of our attention—the World Wide Web (1991) and smartphones (technically IBM in 1992, but come on, the 2007 iPhone) that could do it all: telephone and text, take pictures and video, play music, and surf the by now omnipresent Internet.

This has given rise to a new phenomenon: multiscreening. The media-tracking and analysis company Nielsen gleefully asks in a December 2018 newsletter post: "With all of this technology at consumers' literal fingertips, which of these platforms are they focused on? The answer, in short, is pretty much all of them." This adds up to about ten and a half hours a day that adults spend on TVs, TVs and connected devices, and radio and digital platforms (computer, smartphones, and tablets). That's a hell of a lot of hours! In fact, even if people sleep only six hours a night, this leaves a mere seven and a half hours in which to cram all other activities, including grooming, eating, housework, childcare, errands, and, oh yes, work. So it shouldn't be a revelation that a full 80 percent of Americans do no exercise or recreational sports at all, according to the American Time Use Survey (ATUS). That omission is compounded by the reverential stillness most of us evince when interacting with our beloved apparatuses. We are now more immobile than ever before in human history.

New research shows the damaging effects of sedentarism, sitting or lying for long periods of time. It is slowly being acknowledged as just as much (or even more) of a risk factor as poor diet in obesity and illness. Insufficient physical activity is highly correlated with diabetes, heart disease, high blood pressure, and high cholesterol, risks that are exacerbated when combined with a regular caloric surfeit (weight gain). Over the past two decades, for the first time ever, the rate of all-cause mortality in the United States has increased for adults under the age of 65. In addition to the recent spike in deaths because of the COVID-19 pandemic, some of this comes from the manyfold increase in drug overdoses from opioids; Virginia Commonwealth University School of Medicine researchers calculate some 41,000 additional lost lives. But deaths linked to organ system diseases are also up by 30,000, among them 5,000 from hypertension-related illnesses.

In the past seventy years, U.S. death rates for heart disease and stroke have improved dramatically, thanks to lower smoking rates and improved—and better access to—medical prevention and treatment. In 1950 the death rates per 100,000 for heart disease and stroke were 588.8 and 180.7, respectively; today they are 165 and 37.6 (although, as noted before, these rates are higher than those of our peer countries). We have not made such progress on metabolic diseases—which are, significantly, the ones most sensitive to obesity; the needle has only nudged from 23.1 in 1950 to 21.5 in 2017.

What's the answer?

* * * * *

My parents' approaches to caring for their bodies were polar opposites. As a young man, addled by Beatnik troubadours wailing "500 Miles" and "Freight Train," my father rode the rails. On one trip, he crossed the border to Mexico, probably through El Paso, and found himself walking the line at night after an evening at the cantina. In the dark, he fell off a trestle over a gully, and passed out. He woke up the next morning splayed over a rock and in pain. After that, his back bothered him for the rest of his life. In the late 1960s, when he had a young family and was working as a schoolteacher in a small Vermont town, he took up jogging to cope with the constant discomfort. This, at the time, unheard-of practice elicited crowds of gawking teenagers (his students) and smartass comments from adults such as "What are you running from? Your wife?" But the sport strengthened my father's back

muscles and reduced his spasms. Running 6, 8, 10 miles
(9–16 km) a day became his habit for the next 40 years.

My mother, however, had been a butterball as a young
girl, and while she blossomed into a slim young woman with
a serene gaze and incandescent smile, she waged a battle
with her weight her entire adult life. Although she got some
exercise through housework and gardening, her principal
tool was diet. There were a couple of intense affairs with
Weight Watchers and "health food" à la Francis Moore Lappé
(oh sunflower-seed-studded, honey-sweetened, whole-wheat
cookies of my youth, I remember you still and shudder),
but mostly her approach was to strip any enjoyment from
the food. Small, lean, overcooked pieces of chicken or hamburger, devoid of sauce. Plain, steamed broccoli, squash, or
carrots. Rice and potatoes, unsullied by even a grain of salt.
Despite her punitive approach to victualing, she still gained
weight, at one point topping 200 pounds (90 kg).

I often daydream about making a poster featuring the two
standing side by side naked: my father lean, well-muscled,
and vibrant (although he died relatively young of pancreatic
cancer); my mother bent, heavy, and tired. She was a disease
magnet, starting in her thirties with a brain tumor and then
moving to a stroke, rheumatoid arthritis, and Parkinson's,
all underlain by high blood pressure, high cholesterol, and
atherosclerosis. Her joints hurt, she could hardly walk, and,
during her last five years, lived confined to her bedroom and
our dining room. "Exercises," it would say under my father.
"Doesn't," under my mother.

Long-distance runners, as their friends and families
know all too well, love to humblebrag about their amped-up

metabolisms. "I eat anything I want," they say, sitting across the table from you wolfing down wedges of cake, bowls of pasta, and bags of chips with a winsome smile on their gaunt-cheeked faces. "And I never gain weight!" (Well, of course not, you ninny, you have 1,000 additional calories above baseline to play with.) But while they may like to coyly flaunt their enormous appetites and slim physiques, it's worthwhile to note that no matter what the content of their plates, they almost never suffer from Type 2 diabetes, prediabetes/metabolic syndrome, high cholesterol, high blood pressure, and atherosclerosis. While some runners follow rigorous training diets, others do not. If unhealthy food really were the cause of so many illnesses, at least some of these fitness devotees would suffer from them, too. But they don't.

This is a clue.

It's not our food that's making us sick, but the lack of something endurance athletes have in spades: daily metabolic workouts in which the body must gear up to supply energy at a very high rate. Aerobic exercise shifts the body from its sedentary holding pattern in which its two fuels, glucose and fatty acids, enter cells in their proportion in the bloodstream, to full-steam-ahead operations with a circulation up to four times faster (in nonathletes) and a calorie-burn rate that is four to eight times faster than sitting. In this state, the immense energy needs of heart and muscles are prioritized, and instead of leaving it up to chance, the body tailors the blood's nutrient mix to meet them. Rather than allow molecules to wash through their outer membranes according to the last meal or their fasting-state proportion, cells select which type of energy to consume and send signals so that the bloodstream delivers exactly that. Over time, this process remakes the cardiovascular system and key metabolic pathways, imparting good health.

While there have been some improvements, the overall exercise picture is bleak. CDC data on physical activity in the past decades shows that in 1998, just 14.3 percent of adults met minimum requirements for both aerobic and strengthening activity; by 2017, that had increased to 24.5. But, unfortunately, leisure-time exercise does not compensate for the well-documented loss of activity in other realms of life: work, in which physical occupations have dropped by 83 percent between 1950 and 2000, and transportation, in which the people who walk to work or for errands has declined by 71 percent in the same time period, according to researchers at the St Louis University School of Public Health. Nationally recognized exercise researchers Frank W. Booth and P. Darrell Neufer, in a 2005 article in *American Scientist* argue, "Our underuse of skeletal muscle may play an under-recognized role in the rise of chronic disease as a cause of modern mortality."

I don't eat a family-sized bag of Nacho Doritos every day anymore, although I enjoy potato chips, candy, desserts, and alcohol in moderation. Aside from crackers and cheese, I don't eat a lot of heavily processed foods. But I don't bat an eye when my husband pops a frozen dinner into the microwave or when my daughter cooks up a packet of ramen. (OK, I do bat an eye; those things are sodium bombs.) I avail myself freely of prepared items such as tomato sauce, pasta, boxed pilafs and mixed rices, canned beans and tuna, all

kinds of sauces and condiments, frozen pizza, frozen vegetables and fruits, ice cream and cookies, greens and salads
in a bag, and instant coffee. I'm not fat, and neither is any
member of my family, although Rafi, now in his fifth decade,
sports what he calls *buena vida* around the middle. Not only
that, I'm extraordinarily healthy for my age, or any age, with
a low pulse, good blood pressure, and perfect cholesterol.
This has nothing to do with what I eat—or don't—and
everything to do with the miles I run every day.

CONCLUSION

Just recently my friend Isabella and her husband, Dan, retired from the urban farm they'd managed for more than thirty years, one of a handful remaining in the Boston metropolitan area. On its 100 acres (40 ha), they ran a produce and flower stand, a summer camp, and a Community Supported Agriculture (CSA); held outdoor dinners, fairs, and private events; and led the region's movement for good, fair, and clean food—all while growing season after season of organic and sustainably raised greens, peppers, squashes, melons, berries, and more. Their marriage, second ones for both, is centered on agriculture and food—Isabella's family is Italian; Dan comes from old Vermont small landholders. They looked forward to a quiet domestic life in their New England farmhouse in a town where they are deeply involved in the community, interrupted by occasional travel.

That dream was abruptly upended last summer. During Dan's annual physical, his doctor noticed some scaly patches scattered across his abdomen. Dan hadn't thought anything about them—as someone who spent the day outside, in sun, rain, and sometimes snow, working with his body, he was used to callouses, cuts, bruises, and the occasional rash. But his doctor was worried. He sent Dan for blood tests and a biopsy. The results came back immediately: Dan had a rare type of lymphoma, which had already advanced to stage three. In a blink of an eye, their lives changed. Who knew how much time they had left? Isabella dropped all her outside activities to spend every moment she could with Dan, whether that was eating a meal, taking a walk, or just reading together in bed.

When I visited her recently, Dan was out, attending an agricultural conference. "He has a great attitude," said Isabella. "He hasn't let the diagnosis interfere with all his boards and groups. But he will be on chemotherapy and have to have a weekly blood-washing for the rest of his life." Next week, Dan was scheduled to have the whole surface of his skin treated with radiation. "He looks fine," she said. "But when he takes off his clothes, his entire body is covered with red stripes. He's burning up from inside." A few minutes later the front door banged open, and Dan appeared. He strode into the room and plopped his lanky frame into a dining room chair. Isabella was right; he was just the same as ever. We chatted and eventually I asked him how he was doing. "Fine, fine," he said, brushing off my query to turn the conversation back to the poetry club they are part of and asking me to explain the animal theme in the new book I was about to write. Then, as if he knew I'd been thinking about it the whole time: "One of the risk factors for my cancer is exposure to agricultural chemicals. Know who the only other person I know who has this type of lymphoma? The farm's previous manager."

Many people prefer organic and sustainably raised produce and livestock because they think they are healthier.

As a matter of fact, there is little difference in the nutritional qualities of fruits, vegetables, and grains grown under organic versus conventional conditions. There are greater amounts of residual pesticides and heavy metals, but this has not been shown to adversely affect human health. Some studies have noted an association of reduced cancer risk with organic produce consumption, but it is difficult to separate this benefit from other lifestyle factors that tend to occur simultaneously: higher education, high physical activity levels, and not smoking. Other research has not found a reduced cancer risk at all, including a 2014 British study of more than 623,000 women. The same is true for organically and sustainably raised chickens, turkeys, pigs, and cows.

But this issue isn't just about us. It's about other people—and the planet. And the best way we can protect the health of the people who feed us and the world we live in is to farm organically and sustainably. Twentieth-century agriculture became a miracle of productivity through fossil fuels, the source for synthetic fertilizer, chemical pesticides, and gas to power tractors, combines, planters, and balers. But exposure to these substances has had dire impacts for those who, like my friend Dan, work with them, causing cancers, respiratory diseases, and genetic mutations. Every year, 170,000 agricultural workers around the world die from occupation-related causes; millions more have serious adverse health effects. The same goes for the environment. Poisonous gases, liquids, and dust pollute soil, water, and air and contribute to emissions of carbon and other greenhouse gases. Conventional industrial farming consumes high levels of natural and man-made resources and overwrites complex ecosystems with monocrops. The results contribute to climate change, environmental degradation, and the reduction or even extinction of many species of mammals, birds, reptiles, amphibians, and insects.

To convert to a mostly organic and sustainable system, however, you don't need to revert to the small, subsistence farms of my ancestors. Denmark, which leads the world in the consumption of organic foods, has put in place a new model of green agriculture that can be applied on a large scale, but greatly reduces or eliminates the negative impacts of crops and livestock on pollution. This includes monitoring soil health; crop diversity and rotation; nitrogen-fixing cover crops; natural methods to prevent and control pests, weeds, and diseases; and using vegetation to control erosion. For animals, it means access to the outdoors, both in pens and grazing areas, and no growth hormones or antibiotics except in the case of illness. But the organic sector, which is supported and promoted by the government, also employs science and technology. Robot weeders keep plants free of competitors for moisture and nutrients. Drones assess peak ripeness for harvesting. And microbial agents developed by life science companies are now being used to control diseases rather than chemical pesticides.

"Eating is an agricultural act," wrote Wendell Berry. (Although this curiously overlooks foraging, fishing, and hunting.) It is bound, in unbreakable ways, to the earth and its cultivation and, by extension, to our wise husbandry of the planet. Eating is an agricultural act. But it is also a scientific and technical act. A social, political, and economic act. And even an artistic one. Berry's full stop after his declaration excludes the numerous, often overlapping, other roles food plays in human society—and denies us a multi-dimensional consideration of processed food.

Why can't we take into account that industrial food systems, while imperfect, are a miracle of interconnected functionality, supplying billions of consumers with constant, affordable, safe, and tasty nourishment? Why can't we weigh the fact that food preparation is one of the most onerous daily tasks of a woman's traditional role, contributing to her lack of equality with men? (To not recognize cooking's gendered time burden is itself a form of misogyny.) Why can't we scrutinize the ugly way whole foods are used as a signifier for belonging to an elite socioeconomic class and as a proxy weapon for stigmatizing the poor? Why can't we acknowledge the human, social, and economic costs of encouraging some of our best-prepared young people to enter food-related occupations—in terms of expensive educations wasted, steep declines in rates of traditional altruism, and dim financial futures? And finally, why can't we recognize that our attack on food companies as the cause of national and worldwide increases in obesity is both a gross simplification of a multifactorial problem and perhaps a convenient sideshow in an epic battle among even larger corporate interests (looking at you, pharmaceutical industry)?

Draw your own conclusions. Mine, after exploring processed food's role in each of these different arenas, is that it's fine—perhaps even laudable—to include it as part of our regular daily fare.

APPENDIX

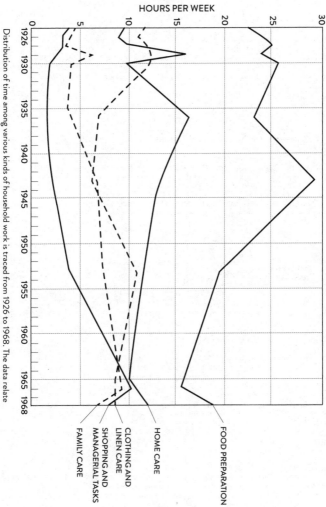

HOURS PER WEEK

Distribution of time among various kinds of household work is traced from 1926 to 1968. The data relate only to nonemployed women, meaning women who did not have full-time jobs outside the household. Top curve includes cleaning up after meals.

FAMILY CARE

SHOPPING AND MANAGERIAL TASKS

CLOTHING AND LINEN CARE

HOME CARE

FOOD PREPARATION

Trends in unpaid care work in the United States

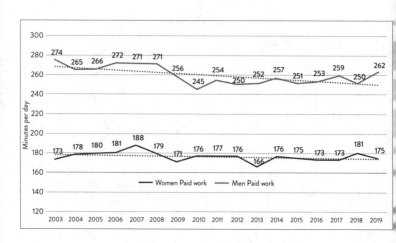

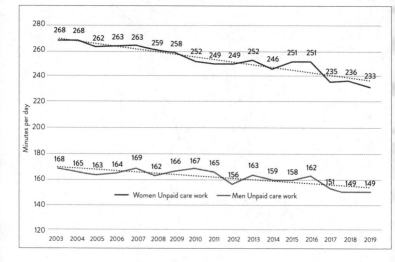

Global trends in total work by sex, 1998 and 2012, 25 countries

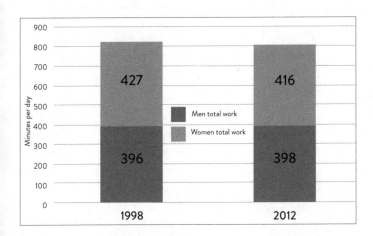

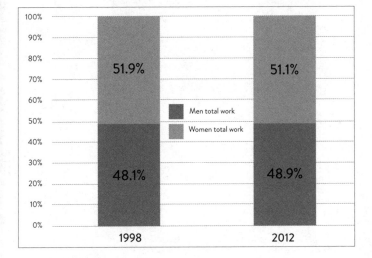

SOURCES

INTRODUCTION

Rosi Scammell, "Pope Francis: Put Away Technology, Enjoy Family Dinners," *Religious News Service,* www.religionnews.com, November 11, 2015.

1 WHAT IS PROCESSED FOOD?

"Farm Groups Urge Rise on 300 Duties," *New York Times* (January 29, 1929), p. 7.

E. W. Lusas and M. N. Riaz, "Soy Protein Products: Processing and Use," *Journal of Nutrition,* cxxv/3, supplement (March 1995), pp. 573s–80s.

Richard V. Oulahan, "Tariff Bill Action Holds Key to End Congress Snarls," *New York Times* (May 27, 1929), p. 1.

Tara Parker-Pope, "Make 2020 the Year of Less Sugar," *New York Times* (December 30, 2019), p. D4.

Jennifer M. Poti, "Development of a Novel Classification System to Determine the Role of Processed and Convenience Foods in the Diets of u.s. Households," unpublished PhD dissertation, University of North Carolina, Chapel Hill, Gillings School of Global Public Health, 2014.

——, Michelle A. Mendez, Shu Wen Ng, and Barry M. Popkin, "Is the Degree of Food Processing and Convenience Linked with the Nutritional Quality of Foods Purchased by u.s. Households?" *American Journal of Clinical Nutrition,* ci (2015), pp. 1251–62.

Panagiotis Sfakianakis and Tzia Constatnina, "Conventional and Innovative Processing of Milk for Yogurt Manufacture; Development of Texture and Flavor: A Review," *Foods (Basel, Switzerland)*, III/1 (March 11, 2014), pp. 176–93.

2 HISTORY OF PROCESSED FOOD AND TWENTY-FIRST-CENTURY INNOVATIONS

Note: This chapter relies primarily on the author's personal knowledge of the subject.

Gustavo Barbosa-Cánovas, interview with the author, March 1, 2016.
Claudia Dziuk O'Donnell, interview with the author, March 25, 2016.
Pedro Fito, "Modelling of Vacuum Osmotic Dehydration of Food," *Journal of Food Engineering*, XXII/1–4 (1994), pp. 313–28.
Kevin Higgins, personal email to the author, March 2, 2016.
Dietrich Knorr and Heribert Watzke, "Food Processing at a Crossroad," *Frontiers in Nutrition*, www.frontiersin.org, June 25, 2019.
John Sedivy, interview with the author, March 3, 2016.

3 AN AGE-OLD TIME SUCK: WOMEN AND COOKING

Arnstein Aassve, Giulia Fuochi, and Letizia Mencarini, "Desperate Housework: Relative Resources, Time Availability, Economic Dependency, and Gender Ideology Across Europe," *Journal of Family Issues*, XXXV/8 (2014), pp. 1000–1022.
American Time Use Survey, U.S. Department of Labor, Bureau of Labor Statistics (various years).
"America's Women and the Wage Gap," National Partnership for Women & Families, www.nationalpartnership.org (September 2019).
Arlene Voski Avakian and Barbara Haber, ed., *From Betty Crocker to Feminist Food Studies: Critical Perspectives on Women and Food*, ebook (Amherst, MA, 2005).
Gabeba Baderoon, "Everybody's Mother Was a Good Cook: Meanings of Food in Muslim Cooking," *Agenda: Empowering Women for Gender Equity*, XVII/51 (2002), pp. 4–15.
Poppy Cannon, *The Can-Opener Cookbook*, ebook (New York, 1951).

Pat Caplan, "'Is It Real Food?' Who Benefits from Globalisation in Tanzania and India?" *Sociological Research Online*, XI/4 (December 1, 2006), pp. 81–93, www.journals.sagepub.com.

Jacques Charmes, "The Unpaid Care Work and the Labour Market: An Analysis of Time Use Data Based on the Latest World Compilation of Time-use Surveys," United Nations, International Labour Organization, www.ilo.org, December 2019.

—, "Time Use Across the World: Findings of a World Compilation of Time Use Surveys," United Nations Development Program (New York, 2015).

David J. Chivers, "Measuring Food Intake in Wild Animals: Primates," *Proceedings of the Nutrition Society*, LVII/2 (1998), pp. 321–32.

Punita Chowbey, "What Is Food Without Love? The Micro-politics of Food Practices Among South Asians in Britain, India, and Pakistan," *Sociological Research Online*, XXII/3 (2017), pp. 165–85, www.journals.sagepub.com.

"Domestic Workers Across the World: Global and Regional Statistics and the Extent of Legal Protection," International Labour Office, www.ilo.org, January 9, 2013.

Francesca Gino, Caroline Ashley Wilmuth, and Alison Woods Brooks, "Compared to men, women view professional advancement as equally attainable, but less desirable," *Proceedings of the National Academy of Sciences*, CXIII/40 (2015), pp. 12354–9.

"Global Gender Gap Report 2014," World Economic Forum, www.weforum.org, October 28, 2014.

"Global Gender Gap Report 2018," World Economic Forum, www.weforum.org, December 17, 2018.

Gottfried Hohmann, "The Diets of Non-Human Primates: Frugivory, Food Processing, and Food Sharing," in *The Evolution of Hominin Diets: Integrating Approaches to the Study of Palaeolithic Subsistence*, ed. Jean-Jacques Hublin and Michael P. Richards, ebook (Dordrecht, 2009).

Muhammad Hussain, Arab Naz, Waseem Khan, Umar Daraz, and Qaisar Khan, "Gender Stereotyping in Family: An Institutionalized and Normative Mechanism in Pakhtun Society of Pakistan," *SAGE Open*, V/3 (2015), pp. 1–11.

Aamir Jamal, "Why He Won't Send His Daughter to School—Barriers to Girls' Education in Northwest Pakistan: A Qualitative Delphi Study of Pashtun Men," *SAGE Open*, VI/3 (2016), pp. 1–14.

Emily Matchar, *Homeward Bound: Why Women Are Embracing the New Domesticity*, ebook (New York, 2013).

Muhammad Aurang Zeb Mughal, "Domestic Space and Socio-spatial Relationships in Rural Pakistan," *South Asia Research*, XXXV/2 (2015), pp. 214–34.

Timo Myllyntaus, "The Entry of Males and Machines in the Kitchen: A Social History of the Microwave Oven in Finland," *Icon*, XVI, special issue, "Technology in Everyday Life" (2010), pp. 226–43.

Ashis Nandy, "The Changing Popular Culture of Indian Food: Preliminary Notes", *South Asia Research*, XXIV/1 (2004), pp. 9–19.

Karen Nussbaum, interview with the author, June 21, 2019.

Margaret Gilpin Reid, *Economics of Household Production* (New York, 1934).

Martha Rosler, "Performance Art: Semiotics of the Kitchen", video file (1975).

"Taking the Lead: Girls and Young Women on the Changing Face of Leadership," Plan International and the Geena David Institute on Gender in Media, www.plan-international.org, June 4, 2019.

Time Use Data Portal, Organization for Economic Cooperation and Development (various years).

Penny Van Esterik, in Ken Albala, series ed., *Food Culture in Southeast Asia* (Westport, CT, 2008).

Joann Vanek, "Time Spent in Housework," *Scientific American*, CCXXXI/5 (1974), pp. 116–21.

Thorstein Veblen, *The Theory of the Leisure Class* [1899], ebook (Salt Lake City, UT, 2008).

Marilyn Waring, interview with the author, June 19, 2019.

Richard Wrangham, *Catching Fire: How Cooking Made Us Human*, ebook (New York, 2009).

Gisele Yasmeen, "Bangkok's Foodscape: Public Eating, Gender Relations, and Urban Change," doctoral thesis, University of British Columbia, 1996.

—, "Plastic-bag Housewives and Postmodern Restaurants: Public and Private in Bangkok's Foodscape," *Urban Geography*, XVII (1996), pp. 526–44.

4 SUBSISTENCE AGRICULTURE CHIC

"100 Years of U.S. Consumer Spending Data for the Nation, New York City, and Boston," U.S. Bureau of Labor Statistics, www.bls.gov, May 2006.

"Agriculture, Forestry, and Fishing, Value Added (% of GDP)," data portal, The World Bank, www.data.worldbank.org, various years.

Wendell Berry, "The Pleasures of Eating," *What Are People For?* (Berkeley, CA, 2010), p. 146.

Ryan Caldbeck, "Beyond Artisanal: How to Grow a Niche Food Business," *Forbes*, www.forbes.com, May 22, 2014.

Carolyn Dimitri, Anne Effland, and Neilson Conklin, "The 20th Century Transformation of U.S. Agriculture and Farm Policy," U.S. Department of Agriculture, Economic Research Service, *Economic Information Bulletin*, 3 (June 2005).

"An Economic Snapshot of the Bedford-Stuyvesant Neighborhood," Office of the New York State Comptroller, www.osc.state.ny.us, September 2017.

"Food Prices and Spending," U.S. Department of Agriculture, Economic Research Service, www.ers.usda.gov, September 20, 2019.

Katy Golvala, "Friday Fast Fact: More Than a Quarter of Bushwick Residents Live Below the Poverty Line," *Bushwick Daily*, www.bushwickdaily.com, July 27, 2018.

Larry Gordon, "Foodie Culture Is Spurring Degree Programs at U.S. Colleges", *Los Angeles Times*, www.latimes.com, November 26, 2015.

"Labor Force Statistics from the Current Population Survey, Table 11b. Employed Persons by Detailed Occupation and Age (2021)," U.S. Bureau of Labor Statistics, www.bls.gov, January 20, 2022.

W. Arthur Lewis, "Economic Development with Unlimited Supplies of Labour," *The Manchester School*, XXII/2 (1954), pp. 139–91.

"Occupational Outlook Handbook (2021)," U.S. Bureau of Labor Statistics, www.bls.gov, September 8, 2022.

Joe Pinsker, "Why Are Millennials So Obsessed With Food?" *The Atlantic*, www.theatlantic.com, August 13, 2015.

"Report of the Expert Group Meeting on 'Strategies for Eradicating Poverty to Achieve Sustainable Development for All,'" United Nations Department of Economic and Social Affairs, Division for Social Policy Development, www.un.org, May 11, 2017.

Klaus Schwab, ed., "The Global Competitiveness Report," World
    Economic Forum, www.weforum.org, 2018.

Tjidde Tempels, Marcel Verweij, and Vincent Blok, "Big Food's
    Ambivalence: Seeking Profit and Responsibility for Health,"
    American Journal of Public Health, CVII/3 (2017), pp. 402–6.

Darrell M. West and Christian Lansang, "Global Manufacturing
    Scorecard: How the U.S. Compares to 18 Other Nations,"
    Brookings Institution, www.brookings.edu, July 10, 2018.

"What is the Average Restaurant Profit Margin? Tips for
    Benchmarking and Optimizing," blog provided by
    https://pos.toasttab.com, accessed November 17, 2017.

"World Fact Book 2017," U.S. Central Intelligence Agency,
    www.cia.gov, accessed September 16, 2022.

5 THE ELEPHANT IN THE ROOM

Frank W. Booth and Darrell P. Neufer, "Exercise Controls Gene
    Expression," *American Scientist*, XCIII/1 (2005), pp. 28–35.

Jennie Brand-Miller and Alan Barclay, "Declining Consumption
    of Added Sugars and Sugar-sweetened Beverages in Australia: A
    Challenge for Obesity Prevention," *American Journal of Clinical
    Nutrition*, CV/4 (2017), pp. 854–63.

George Bray, interview with the author, March 23, 2020.

Center for Science in the Public Interest, "Clean Labels: Public
    Relations or Public Health?" (2017).

James J. DiNicolantonio, Sean C. Lucan, and James H. O'Keefe, "The
    Evidence for Saturated Fat and for Sugar Related to Coronary
    Heart Disease," *Progress in Cardiovascular Diseases*, LVIII/5
    (March–April 2016), pp. 464–72.

"Guideline: Sugars Intake for Adults and Children," World Health
    Organization, www.who.int, March 4, 2015.

Genevieve N. Healy, et al., "Objectively Measured Sedentary Time,
    Physical Activity, and Metabolic Risk," *Diabetes Care*, XXXI/2
    (2008), pp. 369–71.

Ashleigh L. May, David Freedman, Bettylou Sherry, and Heidi M.
    Blanck, "Obesity – United States, 1999–2010," *Morbidity and
    Mortality Weekly Report Supplement*, LXII/3 (2013), pp. 120–28.

The Nielsen Total Audience Report: Q2 2018 (December 2018).

J. Eric Oliver, *Fat Politics: The Real Story Behind America's Obesity Epidemic*, ebook (Oxford, 2005).

Gregory A. Roth, et al., "Global, Regional, and National Burden of Cardiovascular Diseases for 10 Causes, 1990 to 2015," *Journal of the American College of Cardiology*, LXX/1 (2017), pp. 1–25.

Kimber L. Stanhope, "Sugar Consumption, Metabolic Disease and Obesity: The State of the Controversy," *Critical Reviews in Clinical Laboratory Sciences*, LIII/1 (2016), pp. 52–67.

David Stuckler, et al., "Textual Analysis of Sugar Industry Influence on the World Health Organization's 2015 Sugars Intake Guideline," *Bulletin of the World Health Organization*, XCIV/8 (2016), pp. 566–73.

Steven H. Woolf and Heidi Schoomaker, "Life Expectancy and Mortality Rates in the United States, 1959–2017," *Journal of the American Medical Association*, CCCXXII/20 (2019), pp. 1996–2016.

Peter L. Zock, et al., "Progressing Insights into the Role of Dietary Fats in the Prevention of Cardiovascular Disease," *Current Cardiology Reports*, XVIII/11 (2016), pp. 1–13.

CONCLUSION

Julia Baudry, et al., "Association of Frequency of Organic Food Consumption With Cancer Risk: Findings From the NutriNet-Santé Prospective Cohort Study," *JAMA Internal Medicine*, CLXXVIII/12 (2018), pp. 1597–606.

Wendell Berry, "The Pleasures of Eating," *What Are People For?* (Berkeley, CA, 2010).

K. E. Bradbury, et al., "Organic Food Consumption and the Incidence of Cancer in a Large Prospective Study of Women in the United Kingdom," *British Journal of Cancer*, CX/9 (2014), pp. 2321–6.

Danish Agriculture & Food Council, Organic Denmark and Food Nation, ed., "The Organic Way: The Danish Model," Danish Agriculture & Food Council, www.agricultureandfood.dk, accessed September 16, 2022.

Eva Johansson, et al., "Contribution of Organically Grown Crops to Human Health," *International Journal of Environmental Research and Public Health*, XI/4 (2014), pp. 3870–93.

Thi-Hai-Yen Nguyen, et al., "Multiple Exposures and Coexposures to Occupational Hazards Among Agricultural Workers: A Systematic Review of Observational Studies," *Safety and Health at Work*, IX/3 (2018), pp. 239–48.

B. C. Poulsen and D. Jensen, *Abstract Book for the Plant Biologicals Network Annual Symposium, 2018* (Copenhagen, 2018).

FURTHER READING

Berry, Wendell, *What Are People For?* (Berkeley, CA, 2010)

Gaesser, Glenn A., *Big Fat Lies: The Truth About Your Weight and Your Health* (Fawcett, MN, 1996)

Marx de Salcedo, Anastacia, *Combat-Ready Kitchen: How the U.S. Military Shapes the Way We Eat* (New York, 2015)

—, *Eat Like a Pig, Run Like a Horse* (New York and London, 2022)

Matchar, Emily, *Homeward Bound: Why Women Are Embracing the New Domesticity* (New York, 2013)

Pollan, Michael, *In Defense of Food* (New York, 2008)

—, *The Omnivore's Dilemma* (New York, 2006)

Smith, Andrew F., *Fast Food and Junk Food: An Encyclopedia of What We Love to Eat* (Westport, CT, 2011)

Waring, Marilyn, *If Women Counted* (New York, 1988)

Wrangham, Richard, *Catching Fire: How Cooking Made Us Human* (New York, 2009)

ACKNOWLEDGMENTS

No nonfiction book is possible without collaborators, especially those who share their knowledge and experiences. *In Defense of Processed Food* benefits from numerous researchers and experts, but two were especially generous in allowing me to work directly with their students. Dr Robin Kanarek, of Tufts University, enthusiastic about knocking down some hoary shibboleths about food and diet, lent me a group of undergraduates for a semester's project. I thank all of them for helping reveal the heavy burden time in the kitchen is for many women around the world, and that home-cooked meals don't necessarily translate to good health. Dr Barbara Katz Rothman, of the City University of New York, let me commandeer a graduate class in food policy for my own research purposes. I hope the end result helps us all be a little more tough-minded when we analyze the root causes of obesity and noncommunicable diseases.

I am deeply grateful to my publisher, Michael Leaman; series editor, Andrew Smith; and the entire Reaktion staff for their patience, persistence, and attention to detail.

Tables

The author and publishers wish to express their thanks to the sources listed below for table material and/or permission to reproduce it:

Table on page 22–3: Adapted with permission from Table 3.1: Classification system for categorizing foods and beverages based on extent and purpose of processing, and Table 3.2: Classification system for categorizing foods and beverages based on convenience and the amount of preparation. Jennifer M. Poti, "Development of a Novel Classification System to Determine the Role of Processed and Convenience Foods in the Diets of u.s. Households," PhD diss., University of North Carolina at Chapel Hill, 2014; Tables on page 56, 57, 98, 99, 101: Data collection for all tables was done as a 2018 special project by the author with Brita Dawson, Rebecca Moragne, and Afua Ofori-Darko, students of Robin Kanarek, now Professor Emerita of Psychology at Tufts University. The food data was collected from the original sources—usually the national statistics bureau—for the 2015 *Time Use Across the World: Findings of a World Compilation of Time Use Surveys* by economist and statistician Jacques Charmes and published by the United Nations. Health data, with one exception, is from the World Health Organization. Smoking data comes from the World Bank; Table on page 121: Distribution of women's time spent in all care work vs food preparation, 1926–68. Graph created by Graphic Presentation Services, Inc., under contract to *Scientific American*, 1974; Table on page 122: Reprinted with permission. *The Unpaid Care Work and the Labour Market: An Analysis of Time Use Data Based on the Latest World Compilation of Time-use Surveys.* United Nations, International Labour Organization, Geneva (December 2019), Chart 91, p. 116; Table on page 123: Reprinted with permission. *The Unpaid Care Work and the Labour Market: An Analysis of Time Use Data Based on the Latest World Compilation of Time-use Surveys.* International Labour Organization, Geneva (December 2019), Chart 109, p. 133.

INDEX